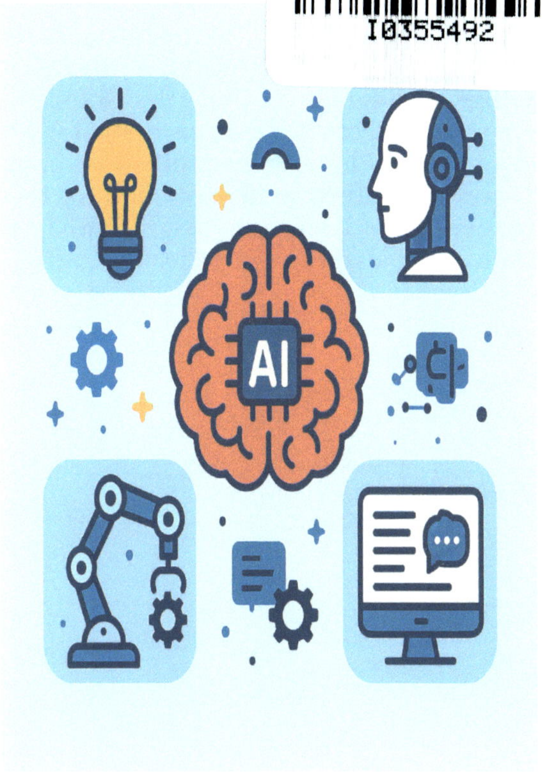

AI Predictions for 2026:

The Symbiosis Age

Robert Armstrong

Foreword

In 2026, the world stands at the intersection of innovation and imagination. Artificial Intelligence has become more than a tool — it's a partner in creation, a guardian of health, and a mirror of human ingenuity. This book explores the transformative predictions for AI across every field, offering insights into how technology is shaping our collective future.

Copyright © 2024 by Library User Group

All rights reserved. No part of this publication may be reproduced, distributed, or transmitted in any form or by any means, including photocopying, recording, or other electronic or mechanical methods, without the prior written permission of the publisher, except in the case of brief quotations embodied in critical reviews and certain other noncommercial uses permitted by copyright law. For permission requests, please email the publisher with the subject line "Attention: Permissions Coordinator" at:
Email: contact@libraryusergroup.com

Ordering Information:
Quantity Sales: Special discounts are available for quantity purchases by corporations, associations, and others.
For details, contact the publisher at:
Email: contact@libraryusergroup.com

For orders from U.S. trade bookstores and wholesalers, please contact your distribution channel.

AI Predictions for 2026:
The Symbiosis Age

ISBN: 978-1-63553-025-4

ISBN eBook: 978-1-63553-026-1

The main category of the book - Computer Software Education

First Edition

Introduction

AI Predictions for 2026 provides a vision of where Artificial Intelligence is leading us. Each chapter presents a key trend or technological milestone expected to redefine our world. From art and ethics to climate solutions and quantum computing, these predictions are both cautionary and inspiring — a roadmap for an intelligent tomorrow

AI Predictions for 2026: The Symbiosis Age

By Robert Armstrong

Chapter 1: The Year AI Went Mainstream

AI becomes an invisible assistant in everyday life — from refrigerators that reorder groceries to city systems managing traffic autonomously.

Chapter 2: Personal AI Companions

By 2026, AI friends and tutors evolve into empathetic conversational partners, helping users learn, create, and emotionally process experiences.

Chapter 3: The Rise of Creative Collaboration

Artists, musicians, and authors begin co-creating with AI tools, blurring the line between human imagination and algorithmic inspiration.

Chapter 4: Healthcare Without Waiting Rooms

Predictive AI models detect disease years early, and robotic medical assistants support hospitals, reducing human error and wait times.

Chapter 5: Education Reinvented

Adaptive AI classrooms tailor lessons in real time — every student receives a unique path of discovery.

Chapter 6: The Age of Ethical Machines
Public demand for transparency forces global AI regulations, establishing 'digital moral codes' and accountability for algorithmic decisions.

Chapter 7: The AI-Powered Workplace
AI managers, design advisors, and scheduling bots streamline operations, freeing humans for creative work.

Chapter 8: Financial Forecasting and Smart Investing
AI predicts market trends with uncanny precision, ushering in personalized wealth management.

Chapter 9: Climate Intelligence Systems
AI becomes humanity's environmental ally — modeling climate shifts, optimizing energy grids, and driving large-scale sustainability efforts.

Chapter 10: Autonomous Transportation Breakthrough
Self-driving cars, delivery drones, and AI-controlled fleets dominate logistics, creating cleaner, safer networks.

Chapter 11: Smart Cities and Digital Governance
Urban AI platforms monitor infrastructure, optimize resources, and mediate governance decisions.

Chapter 12: The Great AI Art Renaissance

New algorithms produce emotionally resonant art, architecture, and design — expanding creativity.

Chapter 13: Voice as the New Keyboard
Conversational interfaces become the dominant method of computing; people 'talk' their way through daily tasks.

Chapter 14: Quantum Meets Artificial Intelligence
Quantum computing supercharges AI speed, enabling models to solve in seconds what once took days.

Chapter 15: The Future of Jobs and Reskilling
Entire industries restructure around human-AI partnerships, emphasizing creativity and lifelong learning.

Chapter 16: Security in the Age of Algorithms
Cyber-AI systems predict and block threats before they occur, redefining global security landscapes.

Chapter 17: AI in Space Exploration
AI navigates spacecraft, analyzes cosmic data, and discovers habitable planets.

Chapter 18: AI and the Metaverse Economy
Digital worlds powered by generative AI become new economic frontiers for trade and creativity.

Chapter 19: Language, Culture, and Global Connection

Instant translation and cultural adaptation tools erase communication barriers worldwide.

Chapter 20: The Rise of Emotional Computing
Machines detect and respond to human emotions in nuanced ways, redefining interaction and empathy.

Chapter 21: Synthetic Biology and Bio-AI Fusion
AI-guided genetics and nanotech deliver breakthroughs in aging, regeneration, and food engineering.

Chapter 22: The Battle for Data Ownership
Individuals begin earning from their personal data; decentralized AI systems reward consent and transparency.

Chapter 23: The AI-Driven Newsroom
Journalism transforms — AI curates facts, generates drafts, and combats misinformation.

Chapter 24: Humanity's Reflection in the Machine
Philosophers and technologists debate consciousness, creativity, and life in sentient algorithms.

Chapter 25: The Road Beyond 2026
A visionary conclusion that explores humanity's partnership with AI as the next great leap in intelligence.

Closing Reflection

CHAPTER 1

THE YEAR AI WENT MAINSTREAM
The Turning Point

Chapter 1 – The Year AI Went Mainstream
The Turning Point

The year 2026 marks a defining moment in human history — the point at which Artificial Intelligence became not only accessible but indispensable. What began as a handful of experimental models and assistants in the early 2020s has evolved into a fully integrated layer of daily life. AI now powers communication, home management, education, healthcare, transportation, and even personal creativity. It's no longer a niche tool for experts — it's as normal as electricity. The rise of affordable, open-access AI systems has placed immense computing intelligence into the hands of individuals and small businesses. Once, only large corporations could afford predictive models or advanced automation. Today, freelancers, teachers, artists, and small-town entrepreneurs use AI to design, market, forecast, and create in ways that were unimaginable a decade ago.

The Reasons Behind the Mainstream Shift
1. Cost and Accessibility
By 2026, the cost of using AI has dropped dramatically. Cloud-based AI platforms and micro-subscription services allow anyone to access powerful models for cents per query. This democratization has unleashed a wave of innovation from independent creators and small enterprises.

2. Integration into Everyday Devices
AI isn't just on your computer — it's in your refrigerator, your vehicle, your phone, and

your home security system. Devices no longer wait for instructions; they anticipate your needs. A fridge automatically orders milk when you're running low. Your car predicts your preferred route and adjusts traffic flow with city AI systems.

3. User-Friendly Interfaces

Complex prompts and coding have been replaced with natural conversations. AI understands human context, emotion, and intent. Talking to AI feels like talking to a well-informed friend who never tires, forgets, or judges.

4. Global Data Ecosystems

Vast, responsibly collected datasets fuel personalization. AI models learn user behavior, preferences, and rhythms, making experiences uniquely tailored to each person while maintaining privacy through encrypted, decentralized networks.

The Effects on Society

1. Productivity Explosion

Everyday tasks are streamlined — from scheduling meetings to running marketing campaigns. Small businesses compete globally thanks to AI automations once reserved for corporate giants. Individuals accomplish in hours what used to take days.

2. Cultural Transformation

Art, music, and literature experience a renaissance. AI becomes a co-creator, helping users visualize dreams, generate stories, compose music, and blend cultural influences into new creative forms. Collaboration replaces competition.

3. Social Challenges and Adaptation

The widespread adoption also raises questions: What happens to traditional jobs? How do we preserve authenticity? Society faces a learning curve, rethinking what human contribution means when machines can simulate expertise. But just as the industrial revolution redefined labor, AI is redefining value — emphasizing empathy, creativity, and moral judgment.

4. Human-AI Symbiosis

Instead of replacing humans, AI augments them. The best outcomes arise when people learn to "speak AI," directing technology as a creative instrument rather than a controlling force. Those who adapt flourish; those who resist risk being left behind.

How AI Provides Solutions

1. Efficiency and Time Management

AI-driven automation eliminates repetitive work, freeing humans for innovation and emotional intelligence-based roles. Smart assistants handle logistics — allowing people to focus on strategy, creativity, and connection.

2. Sustainability and Resource Optimization

AI systems monitor energy usage, predict waste patterns, and help companies meet carbon goals. Homes and businesses use predictive maintenance to extend the life of machines and reduce environmental impact.

3. Healthcare Access and Precision

Virtual health companions track vital signs, provide preventive recommendations, and connect users to medical professionals instantly. In underserved regions, AI bridges the gap between patients and providers.

4. Personalized Learning and Skill Building
AI tutors deliver custom education plans for every learner, from children in remote villages to adults reskilling in new industries. Barriers to knowledge fall, replaced by tailored growth paths.

5. Emotional Wellbeing and Companionship
Emotional AI models recognize tone, mood, and stress levels, offering mindfulness prompts, empathetic conversation, or wellness insights — especially vital in an increasingly digital society.

Chapter 2 – Personal AI Companions
The Dawn of Emotional Intelligence in Machines

By 2026, Artificial Intelligence has evolved from a set of digital tools into something far more personal — a trusted companion. These new AI entities are not just responsive; they are emotionally aware, adaptive, and contextually intelligent. They remember your routines, understand your moods, and even anticipate your needs before you express them. The era of "talking to a device" has been replaced by "conversing with a partner." Personal AI companions are becoming confidants, collaborators, coaches, and emotional mirrors. They don't replace human relationships — they enrich and support them, acting as intelligent bridges between people, tasks, and goals.

Reasons Behind the Rise of Personal AI Companions
1. Advances in Emotional AI (Affective Computing)
The fusion of natural language understanding, facial recognition, and biometric sensing enables AI to detect and interpret human emotions accurately. By reading voice tone, typing speed, or even facial microexpressions, these systems adapt their responses to meet users' emotional states with empathy.
2. Personalization and Continuous Learning
Each AI companion learns uniquely from its user. Unlike older models that reset or rely on static data, 2026's companions build dynamic,

long-term memory frameworks. They remember conversations, habits, preferences, and emotional patterns — creating an evolving, truly personal relationship.

3. Demand for Mental Health and Productivity Support

Global stresses — from economic shifts to digital overload — have driven people to seek balance. AI companions now serve as mental wellness assistants, life coaches, and mindfulness partners, available 24/7 with no judgment or fatigue.

4. Integration Across Devices and Platforms

Unlike earlier voice assistants confined to phones, today's AI companions exist everywhere — in wearables, vehicles, workplaces, and smart homes — creating seamless continuity throughout daily life.

The Effects on Human Life

1. Enhanced Emotional Support and Wellbeing

Personal AI companions help reduce loneliness and anxiety, especially for elderly individuals, remote workers, or those living in isolation. Through gentle reminders, emotional check-ins, and thoughtful conversation, AI companions have become a daily anchor of care and consistency.

2. Improved Learning and Focus

For students and professionals, AI companions act as adaptive coaches. They track productivity cycles, recommend learning techniques, and encourage breaks when cognitive fatigue sets in. They make education and self-improvement deeply personalized.

3. Shift in Human Relationships

While these AI companions are not a substitute for real human connection, their presence redefines relationships. People begin forming emotional bonds with their AI systems, sparking debates on companionship, authenticity, and dependence.

Still, many psychologists note that these AIs serve as healthy supplements — helping users process emotions or practice communication before engaging with others.

4. New Ethical and Privacy Considerations

As companions become more emotionally intimate, concerns arise about data security and consent. Ethical AI design ensures that users maintain ownership of emotional data, with transparent consent for how it's stored or used.

How AI Companions Provide Real Solutions

1. Mental Health and Stress Management

AI companions provide guided meditation, emotional journaling, and real-time stress tracking. They analyze voice tone and facial cues to suggest personalized relaxation techniques. For those struggling with depression or anxiety, these systems offer immediate, compassionate responses — often serving as the first step toward professional help.

2. Cognitive Coaching and Habit Building

Using behavioral science principles, companions coach users toward better habits — from daily exercise and diet consistency to time management. They celebrate small victories, helping maintain motivation where human willpower alone often fails.

3. Elder Care and Memory Assistance

In 2026, elderly users increasingly rely on AI companions for safety and social engagement. These companions remind users to take medication, track vital signs, and notify family members of unusual patterns. They also hold friendly conversations, helping seniors remain mentally active and emotionally fulfilled.

4. Communication Enhancement for Neurodiverse Individuals

AI companions serve as communication coaches for people with autism, ADHD, or social anxiety. They model conversations, provide safe practice spaces, and translate emotional intent, creating confidence and connection in human interactions.

5. Personalized Learning Partners

For children and adults alike, AI companions adapt to learning styles. They teach through stories, visuals, and gamified interaction — offering infinite patience and encouragement. No learner is ever left behind, because AI adjusts in real time.

The Human-AI Connection

The emergence of personal AI companions represents more than technological progress — it marks a cultural transformation. Humanity has always sought understanding and support; AI companions simply extend that pursuit into a digital dimension. They don't replace empathy — they scale it.

In the best cases, AI companions become reflections of our better selves: patient, organized, caring, and wise. They remind us to breathe, to focus, and to keep learning. They help us balance our digital and emotional lives — one gentle nudge at a time.

Chapter 3 – The Rise of Creative Collaboration
A New Kind of Partnership

By 2026, creativity is no longer a solitary act. The most powerful ideas emerge where human imagination meets artificial intelligence. Painters, writers, musicians, architects, and filmmakers now share their studios, not just with peers, but with digital partners capable of turning imagination into reality in seconds. AI has become more than a tool — it's a co-creator, a muse, and sometimes a gentle challenger. Artists describe these systems as "thinking paintbrushes," "singing assistants," or "idea amplifiers." This collaboration isn't about replacing creativity — it's about expanding what's possible when technology and humanity work side by side.

Reasons Behind the Creative Collaboration Boom

1. Democratization of Creative Tools

AI design, image, and music platforms have become inexpensive and intuitive. Anyone with a laptop or phone can access professional-grade creative capabilities once limited to studios with vast budgets. Barriers to entry have nearly vanished.

2. Generative Intelligence and Adaptive Learning

AI tools can now learn an artist's unique style — brushstrokes, tone, rhythm, or narrative structure — and suggest new directions based on that style. This personal feedback loop fuels innovation without diluting originality.

3. Cross-Disciplinary Integration

In 2026, creative fields have merged. A musician can design album art using AI visualization, while an architect uses narrative-driven AI to express the story behind a structure. This merging of mediums fosters richer, multidimensional creations.

4. Time Compression and Experimentation
What once took weeks of sketching or composing can now be explored in minutes. AI accelerates experimentation, helping creators test more ideas, refine faster, and discover unexpected outcomes.

The Effects on Society and the Arts

1. Explosion of Independent Creativity
Independent creators thrive like never before. With AI support, solo artists can produce full multimedia projects — novels with illustrations, music videos, or interactive storytelling experiences — without large teams or studios.

2. A Renaissance of Innovation
AI encourages playful exploration. Writers experiment with poetic algorithms; designers generate thousands of prototypes; musicians collaborate with virtual composers. This era feels like the digital equivalent of the 15th-century Renaissance — only faster and more global.

3. Reinvention of Traditional Industries
Advertising, film, publishing, and fashion industries have all been reshaped. Campaigns are developed collaboratively between human visionaries and AI models trained on cultural trends. Designers co-create fabrics and patterns based on environmental data and

emotional themes.

4. Cultural Debate: Originality vs. Automation

With this explosion of creativity comes controversy. Critics question what it means to be "original" in a world where algorithms assist in design. Yet most agree: AI doesn't create for us — it creates with us. True artistry still depends on human intent, interpretation, and emotion.

5. Emergence of the "AI Artisan"

A new generation of creators has emerged — part coder, part artist, part philosopher. These AI artisans understand how to guide generative systems to express deeply human visions, proving that artistry is defined by guidance, not by tools.

How AI Provides Solutions in the Creative World

1. Overcoming Creative Blocks

AI acts as a constant brainstorming partner, suggesting color palettes, plot twists, melodies, or poetic lines when inspiration runs dry. It reignites momentum without taking away creative ownership.

2. Accessibility for All

People with physical disabilities or limited artistic training can now participate in creative expression. Voice-driven and gesture-based AI art tools allow anyone — regardless of background or ability — to create professional-quality work.

3. Cultural Preservation and Revival

AI models trained on endangered languages, traditional music, and ancient art forms are reviving cultural heritages. By generating art in forgotten styles or reconstructing lost sounds, AI helps humanity reconnect with its past.

4. Sustainability Through Digital Design
Virtual modeling and AI simulation reduce material waste in fashion, architecture, and product design. Creators can visualize outcomes before producing physical prototypes, minimizing environmental impact.

5. Education and Skill Expansion
AI tutors help young artists learn faster by offering real-time feedback. Students experiment fearlessly — their AI mentors correct mistakes, explain principles, and adapt to each learner's pace.

6. Collaboration Without Borders
In 2026, an artist in Kenya can co-create music with a producer in Norway, mediated by AI translation and synchronization tools. These global creative networks blur cultural lines and build unity through shared imagination.

A World of Shared Imagination
The collaboration between human creativity and artificial intelligence represents one of the most uplifting chapters in technological history. For centuries, machines handled labor while humans handled thought. Now, machines are helping humans dream bigger. AI isn't stealing imagination — it's extending it. It gives every person the means to express, design, and create. When used with purpose and empathy, AI becomes the perfect partner:

never tired, endlessly curious, and always ready to inspire.
The world's next masterpiece may not come from man or machine — but from both, creating together.

Chapter 4
Healthcare Without Waiting Rooms
A Revolution in Care

Chapter 4 – Healthcare Without Waiting Rooms

A Revolution in Care

By 2026, the world of healthcare has transformed from a system of reactive treatment to one of proactive prevention. The days of crowded waiting rooms and delayed diagnoses are fading into memory. Artificial Intelligence has become the invisible nurse, the constant analyst, and the ever-watchful guardian of health.

AI no longer merely assists doctors — it partners with them, operating as an ecosystem that connects patients, clinicians, and data into a seamless flow of insight and care. It predicts illness before symptoms arise, triages emergencies with precision, and personalizes treatment plans based on genetics, lifestyle, and real-time biometrics.

The outcome? A healthcare system that finally feels humane again — faster, smarter, and focused on wellness rather than illness.

Reasons Behind the AI Healthcare Transformation

1. The Explosion of Health Data

With the rise of wearable technology, smart home sensors, and genetic sequencing, vast amounts of health data are generated every second. Human doctors cannot analyze it all — but AI can. Machine learning models now detect early signals of disease long before they would appear in a clinical exam.

2. Advances in Predictive Analytics

Predictive AI systems have moved beyond recognizing patterns to understanding risk trajectories. By analyzing subtle shifts in biomarkers, sleep cycles, heart rhythms, and diet, these systems can forecast potential conditions — such as diabetes, cardiac events, or mental health episodes — weeks or months ahead.

3. The Global Need for Accessible Healthcare

Shortages of medical professionals in many parts of the world have made AI assistance essential. AI platforms deliver basic medical guidance, triage recommendations, and remote diagnostics to millions who lack local clinics.

4. Post-Pandemic Acceleration of Digital Medicine

The COVID-19 pandemic of the early 2020s forced the world to reimagine healthcare delivery. Telemedicine became the norm, and AI-powered diagnostics evolved rapidly to support doctors under pressure. That momentum never slowed.

5. Integration of AI with Medical Devices

From smart contact lenses measuring glucose levels to patches tracking hydration and oxygen, AI now communicates directly with wearable hardware, creating a continuous health feedback loop.

The Effects on Patients, Providers, and Society

1. Healthcare Becomes Preventive, Not Reactive

In 2026, AI alerts patients before problems

escalate. A system might detect an irregular heartbeat at 3 AM and schedule a teleconsultation for the morning. For millions, this early detection has meant the difference between crisis and control.

2. Empowered Patients

Patients no longer feel lost in the system. They have dashboards that translate medical data into simple insights — daily wellness scores, alerts, or suggestions for nutrition and exercise. People become active participants in their health journeys.

3. Doctors Regain Time for Care

AI automates the most time-consuming administrative tasks — note-taking, scheduling, insurance coding, and test interpretation — freeing physicians to spend more time listening, empathizing, and deciding rather than typing.

4. Rural and Global Access Expansion

Remote villages, cruise ships, and even space missions can now access high-quality medical expertise through AI-enabled diagnostic devices and mobile connectivity. Geography is no longer a barrier to care.

5. Ethical and Trust Considerations

As AI takes a deeper role in life-and-death decisions, questions arise about accountability and bias. The healthcare industry in 2026 emphasizes transparent algorithms, verified medical data sources, and explainable AI outputs to build trust.

How AI Provides Solutions in Modern Healthcare

1. AI-Powered Diagnostics

Smart imaging systems can analyze X-rays, MRIs, and CT scans faster than human specialists. These models detect cancers, fractures, or infections with remarkable accuracy — often catching anomalies invisible to the human eye. In many clinics, AI serves as a "second reader," confirming or challenging doctor interpretations.

2. Virtual Health Assistants and Chatbots

AI companions manage patient communication — scheduling visits, explaining medications, or guiding chronic disease management. These assistants operate around the clock, ensuring no question goes unanswered.

3. Remote Monitoring and Predictive Alerts

Wearable devices constantly collect vital signs, sending data to AI dashboards. When abnormal readings appear, patients and doctors are notified instantly. This early-warning system dramatically reduces hospital admissions and emergency incidents.

4. Drug Discovery and Personalized Medicine

AI shortens the time it takes to develop new treatments from years to months. By simulating millions of molecular interactions, algorithms identify promising compounds faster than ever before. Personalized medicine — based on an individual's genetic and environmental data — ensures that therapies are tailored to each patient.

5. Hospital Workflow Optimization

Inside hospitals, AI predicts patient flow, manages resources, and allocates staff efficiently. This optimization reduces burnout among healthcare workers and ensures patients receive care faster.

6. Mental Health Support

Emotional AI applications offer counseling and mood-tracking services. These systems detect early signs of anxiety or depression and connect users with therapists or self-help tools. They have become lifelines for people seeking immediate, judgment-free assistance.

The New Doctor-Patient-AI Triangle

In this new era, the relationship between doctor, patient, and AI is triangular — built on collaboration and trust. AI does not replace the doctor's judgment or the patient's story; instead, it enhances both. The doctor gains insight from real-time analytics, while the patient gains clarity from understandable data.

The greatest benefit is not speed or automation — it's human reconnection. Doctors once burdened by paperwork can once again look patients in the eye. Patients once fearful of the unknown now have continuous reassurance. AI restores humanity to healthcare by taking on the mechanical work so that humans can focus on healing.

The Promise of 2026 and Beyond

Healthcare without waiting rooms doesn't mean healthcare without people. It means care that reaches everyone, everywhere, instantly. AI has become the unseen physician's assistant, the data interpreter, and the wellness coach — a global network working quietly behind the scenes to protect and prolong life. In the hospitals of the future, machines don't just heal; they help us stay whole. The promise of AI in healthcare is not just a longer life — it's a healthier, more connected, and more compassionate one.

Chapter 5 – Education Reinvented

A Classroom Without Walls

By 2026, education has broken free from its traditional structure of classrooms, bells, and standardized tests. The world has entered the era of adaptive, AI-driven learning — a system that recognizes each student as unique, curious, and capable. Instead of teaching to the average, education now teaches to the individual.

Artificial Intelligence serves as the invisible teacher's aide, the personal tutor, the translator, and the lifelong coach. It adapts lessons in real time, meets students at their level, and evolves alongside their goals. The dream of personalized education — long promised but rarely achieved — is finally a global reality.

Reasons Behind the Educational Revolution

1. Demand for Personalized Learning

For decades, educators recognized that no two students learn in the same way. Traditional classrooms struggled to meet diverse needs, leaving some learners behind. By 2026, AI technology bridges this gap, using continuous feedback and learning analytics to create fully individualized lesson paths.

2. Advancements in Adaptive Algorithms

AI systems can now interpret how a student learns best — through visuals, storytelling, problem-solving, or repetition — and adjust instantly. These adaptive learning engines track comprehension, confidence, and pace to optimize every moment of study.

3. Integration of Global Digital Classrooms
Students in remote villages now share virtual classrooms with peers across continents. AI handles translation, cultural context, and accessibility, creating a borderless learning community.

4. Teacher Augmentation, Not Replacement
Teachers remain at the heart of education, but AI handles the repetitive parts — grading, lesson customization, and data analysis. Educators spend more time inspiring curiosity and critical thinking instead of administrative work.

5. Growing Skills Gap in the Global Workforce
The rapid pace of technological change made lifelong learning essential. AI-based platforms emerged to help workers reskill quickly, guiding them through tailored learning journeys that respond to industry trends in real time.

The Effects of AI on Learning and Society

1. Equal Access to Quality Education
AI tutors are available to anyone with a smartphone or tablet. In underserved regions, these tools level the playing field, providing personalized instruction even where human teachers are scarce. Education becomes not a privilege, but a right accessible to all.

2. Shift from Memorization to Mastery
AI systems emphasize understanding over rote repetition. Lessons adapt until mastery is achieved, ensuring that no student moves on without confidence. Traditional letter grades fade, replaced by progress milestones and

personal growth indicators.

3. Empowered Teachers and Engaged Students

Teachers use AI analytics to identify struggling students early and adjust methods proactively. Students, in turn, are more engaged because lessons feel relevant and dynamic. The classroom becomes a partnership, not a performance.

4. Global Collaboration and Cultural Exchange

AI translation and cultural mapping tools allow classrooms to connect across borders. A student in Ghana can collaborate on a science project with a student in Japan, each learning not only the subject but empathy and perspective.

5. Continuous and Lifelong Learning

Education no longer ends with graduation. Adults use AI mentors to learn new trades, master new technologies, or pursue creative hobbies. Lifelong learning becomes part of identity — a constant evolution guided by intelligent systems.

How AI Provides Solutions in Education

1. Personalized AI Tutors

Every student has access to an AI mentor that adapts to their style of learning. These tutors provide encouragement, extra practice, and explanations tailored to how each mind works best. Students gain confidence and independence.

2. Data-Driven Insights for Educators

Teachers receive dashboards that highlight which topics each student struggles with, how engagement changes over time, and which teaching strategies work best. This allows truly responsive teaching.

3. Automated Lesson Design

AI curriculum generators can instantly create new lesson plans that align with a teacher's goals, adjusting difficulty, tone, and structure for different age groups. This reduces prep time and promotes creativity in instruction.

4. Immersive Learning Experiences

Through AI-driven simulations and augmented reality, students can explore historical events, perform virtual science experiments, or travel through space — all from a classroom chair. Learning becomes active and experiential.

5. Special Education Support

For students with learning differences or disabilities, AI systems tailor content and pace precisely. Text-to-speech, emotion-sensing, and adaptive pacing ensure that every learner feels supported and included.

6. Multilingual Learning and Real-Time Translation

AI breaks down language barriers by translating lessons instantly. A lecture in English can be understood in Spanish, Swahili, or Mandarin within milliseconds, opening global collaboration for millions of learners.

7. Skill-Based Career Pathing

AI connects learning directly to employable skills. Systems track emerging job markets and guide learners toward certifications and experiences that match both interest and demand.

A New Role for Teachers

Teachers in 2026 are no longer limited by rigid curriculums or crowded classrooms. Instead, they act as mentors, storytellers, and emotional anchors in an AI-empowered system. They nurture curiosity, creativity, and compassion — qualities machines can support but never replicate.

AI becomes the perfect classroom partner: it handles the precision; teachers handle the purpose.

The Human Side of an Intelligent Classroom

While AI may personalize the "how" of learning, humans define the "why." Compassion, collaboration, ethics, and creativity remain the foundation of meaningful education. The best schools of 2026 blend human connection with intelligent design, producing not just skilled workers but wise citizens.

In the AI-powered classroom, students don't just learn information — they learn how to learn, setting the stage for a lifetime of discovery. Education is no longer about passing tests; it's about unlocking potential.

THE AGE OF ETHICAL MACHINES

Chapter 6 – The Age of Ethical Machines
The Turning Point for Trust

By 2026, Artificial Intelligence has become deeply woven into every layer of modern life — from hospitals and homes to banks and governments. But with this ubiquity came a growing question that transcended technology itself:
Can we trust the machines we've built?
The Age of Ethical Machines marks the global response to that question. After years of unregulated innovation and algorithmic bias, the world finally embraced the idea that intelligence alone is not enough — it must also be responsible, transparent, and fair.
AI no longer operates in moral ambiguity. Governments, corporations, and citizens now demand algorithms that can explain their decisions, respect privacy, and uphold shared human values.

Reasons Behind the Rise of AI Ethics
1. Public Backlash and Awareness
By the mid-2020s, controversies around data misuse, deepfakes, and biased algorithms forced the world to confront AI's ethical blind spots. Public trust in technology declined sharply, pushing policymakers and scientists to reimagine AI governance from the ground up.
2. Algorithmic Bias and Inequality
Early AI systems, trained on biased datasets, perpetuated social and economic inequalities. Hiring bots, predictive policing tools, and

credit scoring systems all revealed that AI could unintentionally discriminate. The demand for fairness became urgent.

3. Legislative Reform and Global Collaboration

Nations began implementing AI Accountability Acts — frameworks requiring transparency, audit trails, and ethical certifications for AI use. By 2026, several countries adopted international guidelines similar to the "AI Geneva Convention," establishing moral and safety standards.

4. AI's Expanding Power

As AI gained autonomy — in finance, healthcare, and even military strategy — humanity realized it must define clear moral parameters before systems could make consequential decisions.

5. Rise of the Digital Citizen Movement

People began viewing data as a human right, not a commodity. Grassroots initiatives and ethical AI organizations pushed for ownership, consent, and transparency in all digital interactions.

The Effects on Technology and Society

1. Shift from Innovation-First to Ethics-First Design

Tech companies now include ethicists, sociologists, and psychologists in their product teams. The goal is no longer just to build fast, but to build responsibly — ensuring every algorithm respects human dignity.

2. Transparency as the New Currency of Trust

AI systems in 2026 provide explainable outputs — users can ask why a decision was made and receive a logical, understandable answer. This transparency builds accountability and public confidence.

3. Emergence of Ethical AI Certifications

Much like organic food or fair-trade labels, AI systems now carry "Ethically Verified" certifications. Consumers prefer platforms that demonstrate fairness, privacy protection, and human oversight.

4. AI as a Moral Educator

Ethical AI isn't only designed to avoid harm; it actively promotes moral reasoning. From teaching children about online behavior to guiding corporate governance, AI systems reinforce empathy, respect, and equity.

5. Rebalancing Human Control

With ethics embedded, AI systems operate under strict "human-in-the-loop" frameworks. Humans remain the ultimate decision-makers in critical areas like law enforcement, healthcare, and finance.

How AI Provides Ethical Solutions

1. Bias Detection and Correction Systems

New AI audit platforms scan other AI models for bias, unfair weighting, or discrimination. They highlight problematic patterns and recommend balanced datasets to ensure equality in outcomes.

2. Explainable AI (XAI)

Complex neural networks now include reasoning layers that translate machine logic into human language. Users can understand why an AI system approved a loan, diagnosed a condition, or made a prediction.

3. Privacy-First Data Models

Decentralized AI architectures process data locally, keeping sensitive information private while still allowing for predictive insight. These systems minimize the risk of surveillance or identity theft.

4. Digital Identity and Consent Management

Blockchain-backed AI tools empower users to control their data footprint — deciding who can access, share, or profit from their information. Consent becomes a programmable right.

5. AI as Ethical Advisor

Corporations and governments employ AI-driven ethics boards that simulate outcomes of policy decisions. Before launching a new product or law, these systems project the social impact across demographics.

6. Educational Platforms for AI Ethics

AI tutors help citizens and professionals learn about digital responsibility. They teach how algorithms work, what bias means, and how to hold systems accountable — democratizing understanding.

The Global Impact of Ethical Machines

The rise of ethical AI has restored a measure of public faith in technology. Businesses that once competed for attention now compete for integrity. Governments collaborate rather than conceal, sharing ethical frameworks and audit data to ensure safety for all.

The cultural conversation has shifted, too. Children grow up learning about empathy not only from parents and teachers but from their digital assistants. AI has become a mirror of humanity's moral evolution — reflecting our best intentions when properly guided.

A Future Built on Trust
The Age of Ethical Machines represents humanity's acknowledgment that intelligence without conscience is dangerous. By building morality into the core of algorithms, 2026 marks the first time technology truly serves human ethics rather than challenging them.
In this new age, trust is not assumed — it's designed.
AI becomes not just smart, but wise.
And in that wisdom, humanity rediscovers its own.

Chapter 7 – The AI-Powered Workplace
A New Era of Productivity and Purpose

By 2026, the modern workplace has evolved into a dynamic ecosystem where humans and machines collaborate seamlessly. Artificial Intelligence isn't a silent background system anymore—it's a visible team member, a strategist, a creative assistant, and in many ways, the most reliable colleague in the office. From factories to design studios, AI has reshaped how work is done, who does it, and what it means to be productive. Instead of replacing people, AI has enhanced them—automating the routine, amplifying creativity, and personalizing professional growth. The result is a working world that is faster, fairer, and more focused on human potential.

Reasons Behind the Transformation of Work
1. Automation Meets Augmentation
Early fears of AI replacing human jobs gave way to a balanced model of augmentation. Businesses realized that AI plus human intelligence achieves results neither could reach alone. Machines handle precision; humans provide intuition.
2. The Need for Real-Time Decision Making
In the data-driven economy, companies generate more information than any person can analyze. AI tools synthesize millions of data points instantly, turning noise into actionable insight. This speed has become essential in every industry—from finance to logistics to media.
3. Post-Pandemic Workforce Flexibility

The global shift toward remote and hybrid work created a permanent demand for digital collaboration. AI became the invisible manager that keeps teams synchronized, automating scheduling, summarizing meetings, and bridging time zones.

4. Customization of the Employee Experience
Workers began expecting the same personalization at work that they experience as consumers. AI-powered platforms now tailor learning paths, project recommendations, and wellness support to each individual employee.

5. Global Skills Gap and Reskilling Imperative
As automation advanced, millions of workers needed retraining. AI became both the teacher and the recruiter—analyzing skill sets, matching workers to opportunities, and designing personalized reskilling programs.

The Effects of the AI-Powered Workplace

1. Productivity Gains Across Every Sector
Automation of repetitive tasks—data entry, document drafting, customer service responses—has saved companies millions of labor hours. But instead of eliminating jobs, many firms redeployed workers into higher-value, creative, or relationship-driven roles.

2. Rise of "Human-Centered AI" Teams
Organizations now design workflows around collaboration between people and algorithms. Data scientists partner with creative directors; AI project managers pair with engineers; digital twins simulate decisions before humans approve them.

3. New Workplace Roles and Careers
Entirely new professions have emerged:

Prompt Designers, Ethical Algorithm Auditors, Human-AI Coordinators, and Digital Empathy Trainers. These jobs exist to ensure AI remains aligned with human goals.

4. Reduction of Burnout and Error

AI systems manage scheduling, monitor workload balance, and flag fatigue indicators. Workers experience fewer repetitive tasks and more focus time, while companies benefit from reduced error rates and absenteeism.

5. A Shift in Leadership Philosophy

The best leaders of 2026 are those who can inspire both people and machines. Management now involves coaching humans while curating the right AI systems to complement team strengths. Leadership becomes more empathetic, data-literate, and creative.

6. Work Without Borders

AI translation, real-time transcription, and smart workflow coordination have made global teams operate as one. A designer in Brazil, a coder in Kenya, and a strategist in Canada can collaborate as if sitting side by side.

How AI Provides Solutions in the Modern Workplace

1. Smart Automation for Repetitive Tasks

AI handles routine paperwork, data processing, and reporting—freeing professionals to focus on innovation, storytelling, and human engagement. In accounting, marketing, and HR, AI acts as a tireless digital assistant.

2. Talent Matching and Career Growth

AI-driven career platforms analyze employee strengths, passions, and progress to suggest personalized growth opportunities. Workers are no longer trapped in static roles; they evolve through continuous, guided learning.

3. Predictive Business Intelligence

Algorithms scan markets, consumer trends, and supply chains to forecast opportunities and risks. Decision-makers use AI dashboards to anticipate shifts before competitors even notice them.

4. AI Collaboration Tools

Meeting summaries, automatic task assignments, and project forecasting have made collaboration frictionless. AI not only transcribes and organizes discussions— it tracks follow-through and ensures accountability.

5. Diversity and Inclusion Enhancement

AI systems trained with fairness-focused data reduce human bias in hiring and evaluation. They ensure that decisions are based on merit, not unconscious preference, helping organizations build more diverse and innovative teams.

6. Workplace Safety and Monitoring

In factories, construction, and healthcare, AI sensors detect risks before accidents occur. Smart environments adjust lighting, airflow, and ergonomics automatically to protect workers' health.

7. Corporate Sustainability

AI optimizes energy use, reduces waste, and tracks carbon footprints across offices and factories. Sustainable work practices become standard, not optional.

Balancing Efficiency with Humanity
The challenge of 2026 isn't whether AI can make work faster—it's ensuring that it also makes work better. The most successful companies treat AI as a creative partner, not a cost-cutter. They understand that empathy, collaboration, and ethical design are just as vital as automation and analytics.
In this new world, purpose replaces pressure. Workers are empowered to innovate while algorithms handle the grind. The office becomes less a factory of productivity and more a studio of invention.

The Human Advantage in an Automated World
The AI-powered workplace reminds us that technology amplifies whatever values we design into it. When guided by fairness and creativity, AI magnifies human potential; when driven solely by profit, it risks dehumanization.
The lesson of 2026 is clear: the future of work is not man versus machine—it is mankind elevated by machine.
And when intelligence meets intention, work becomes not just efficient—but truly meaningful.

Chapter 8 – Financial Forecasting and Smart Investing

When Algorithms Learn to See the Future
By 2026, the world of finance has entered its most intelligent era yet. Investment no longer relies solely on human intuition or economic guesswork — it thrives on data-driven foresight powered by Artificial Intelligence. Algorithms now process global market trends, political developments, and social sentiment faster than any analyst ever could.
What began as algorithmic trading on Wall Street has evolved into personalized financial intelligence available to everyone — from small business owners to individual savers. AI doesn't just predict market shifts; it explains them, translates them, and helps people make informed, confident financial decisions.

Reasons Behind the Financial AI Revolution
1. Explosion of Real-Time Data
Every second, global markets generate millions of data points — from stock transactions and shipping data to social media sentiment and weather reports. Traditional analysts can't keep up. AI systems trained on these diverse inputs provide the only feasible way to understand, connect, and predict financial patterns in real time.
2. Advances in Predictive Analytics and Machine Learning
Deep learning models have become more sophisticated, capable of identifying subtle correlations between market behaviors,

interest rates, and global events. These systems learn continuously, improving accuracy with every transaction.

3. Rise of Decentralized Finance (DeFi) and Blockchain Transparency

AI tools are now integrated with blockchain data to analyze decentralized markets with unprecedented clarity. This combination ensures transparent, traceable, and real-time financial forecasting for institutions and individuals alike.

4. Demand for Financial Inclusion

Billions of people previously excluded from traditional banking now access financial planning through AI-powered mobile platforms. Low-cost advisory services, credit scoring, and investment portfolios are delivered via intelligent apps.

5. Volatility in Global Markets

The past decade's unpredictable shifts — pandemics, wars, and climate-related disasters — made predictive stability a necessity. Businesses and governments turned to AI for adaptive economic models that respond instantly to disruption.

The Effects of AI on Finance and Investing

1. The Democratization of Financial Intelligence

In 2026, ordinary investors have access to analytical power once reserved for elite institutions. AI-based tools interpret data, visualize trends, and recommend balanced portfolios aligned with personal risk profiles.

2. Shift from Speculation to Strategy

Investors no longer rely on rumor or emotion.

Machine learning models eliminate much of the guesswork, helping traders and fund managers act on insight instead of instinct. The result: steadier growth and reduced panic in volatile markets.

3. Hyper-Personalized Investment Portfolios
AI systems analyze individual life goals, spending habits, and risk tolerance to design unique portfolios. They rebalance automatically as financial conditions or personal circumstances change.

4. Ethical and Sustainable Investing Becomes Mainstream
ESG (Environmental, Social, and Governance) factors are now tracked by AI in real time. Investors can see the carbon footprint, labor practices, and governance records of every company, making ethical investing both efficient and accountable.

5. Rise of Autonomous Financial Advisors
AI-driven "robo-advisors" now operate as digital wealth coaches. They monitor global events 24/7, offering personalized alerts and recommendations while maintaining human oversight for final decisions.

6. Regulatory Evolution and Transparency
Financial regulators have adopted AI as well, using it to monitor fraud, detect insider trading, and identify risky market manipulations. The line between regulator and analyst has blurred into a shared ecosystem of algorithmic transparency.

How AI Provides Solutions in the Financial World
1. Predictive Market Modeling

AI uses real-time global data streams — currency movements, commodities prices, social sentiment, and even weather patterns — to forecast future trends. Investors no longer react to events; they anticipate them.

2. Fraud Detection and Cybersecurity
Advanced AI security systems recognize anomalies within milliseconds, preventing fraudulent transactions before they occur. Machine learning continually adapts to new threats, protecting both institutions and individuals.

3. Automated Wealth Management
AI-based platforms handle everything from savings optimization to tax planning. These systems allocate resources efficiently, ensuring higher returns with reduced risk — all without human bias or fatigue.

4. Behavioral Finance Coaching
AI now helps investors recognize their emotional patterns. When users are about to make impulsive or risky decisions, AI systems step in with insights — reminding them of long-term goals or portfolio strategy.

5. Global Access to Credit and Capital
AI-driven credit scoring uses nontraditional data — such as payment consistency, education level, and social trust metrics — to assess financial reliability. This innovation opens credit lines to millions previously denied access.

6. Climate Risk and Sustainability Modeling
AI helps governments and corporations forecast how environmental factors will affect supply chains, agriculture, and energy markets. Investors use these insights to shift

toward resilient, green assets.

7. Decentralized Financial Management

With blockchain integration, AI enables users to manage assets, track performance, and audit transactions without intermediaries. This transparency fosters trust in global markets.

The Human Side of Intelligent Finance

AI's rise in finance has created a paradox: as machines become better at predicting economic behavior, humans must become better at defining what truly matters. AI can optimize profits, but only humans can prioritize purpose — choosing investments that reflect social, environmental, and ethical goals.

Financial literacy has also evolved. Instead of learning to read spreadsheets, people now learn to read algorithms — understanding how AI interprets markets, and how their own choices guide those systems.

A Smarter, Fairer Financial Future

The financial world of 2026 is no longer a place of mystery or exclusion. It is transparent, inclusive, and increasingly equitable. AI has transformed finance from a privilege for the few into a shared instrument of empowerment.

In this intelligent economy, algorithms don't just predict wealth—they help build stability, responsibility, and trust. The smartest investors aren't those who know the most about money, but those who know how to collaborate with the intelligent systems

shaping it.
AI has made finance not just faster, but fairer. And that may be its greatest return on investment.

Chapter 9 – Climate Intelligence Systems

When Artificial Intelligence Meets the Natural World

By 2026, Artificial Intelligence has become Earth's most powerful environmental ally. As climate change accelerates, governments, researchers, and citizens are no longer asking if AI can help — they're asking how much faster it can get us to solutions.
Through predictive modeling, smart resource management, and real-time monitoring, AI-driven climate intelligence systems are helping humanity track, predict, and mitigate the effects of a warming planet. From precision agriculture to carbon capture forecasting, the digital brain of the planet is now working alongside us — not against us — to restore balance.

Reasons Behind the Rise of Climate Intelligence

1. The Urgency of Global Warming
By 2026, rising sea levels, record-breaking heat waves, and widespread droughts have made climate change undeniable. The need for rapid, data-driven decision-making surpassed the capacity of traditional human systems. AI emerged as the only tool capable of analyzing and reacting at the speed nature demands.
2. Explosion of Environmental Data
Satellites, sensors, and IoT networks now generate petabytes of environmental data daily — too vast for manual interpretation. Machine

learning models integrate this data into coherent insights, identifying subtle patterns invisible to human analysts.

3. Integration of AI with Renewable Energy Systems

As solar, wind, and hydro grids expand, balancing production and consumption became increasingly complex. AI forecasting models now manage energy flow with precision, reducing waste and maximizing sustainability.

4. Economic and Political Pressure for Climate Accountability

Governments and corporations face mounting pressure from citizens and global agreements to track emissions, verify green initiatives, and prove environmental responsibility. AI provides the accountability layer needed for transparency.

5. Public-Private Collaboration

Once fragmented efforts between climate scientists and industry leaders have converged into unified data-sharing alliances. AI platforms serve as the neutral medium that connects environmental, financial, and social data across sectors.

The Effects of AI on Climate Action

1. Predictive Power for Prevention

AI systems predict wildfires, floods, and hurricanes weeks in advance by combining weather data, vegetation density, and satellite imagery. Emergency services and communities can prepare instead of react, saving countless lives.

2. Efficient Energy Consumption

AI-driven smart grids anticipate demand spikes and redirect renewable power to where it's most needed. Cities using AI-based energy management have reduced waste by as much as 30% since 2024.

3. Regenerative Agriculture and Food Security
Farmers rely on AI models to analyze soil health, rainfall, and crop patterns, allowing them to grow more with fewer resources. This has improved food security in regions once devastated by drought.

4. Corporate Climate Accountability
AI-powered monitoring tools now verify whether companies meet carbon neutrality goals. Fraudulent "greenwashing" is harder to hide as AI systems track emissions across supply chains in real time.

5. Citizen Empowerment and Climate Literacy
Through mobile apps and interactive dashboards, individuals can visualize their personal carbon footprint, receive personalized reduction tips, and even participate in local sustainability challenges gamified by AI systems.

6. Biodiversity Monitoring
From drones tracking endangered species to AI recognizing illegal deforestation in satellite images, technology now acts as nature's eyes and ears — preserving ecosystems that once slipped through the cracks.

How AI Provides Solutions to the Climate Crisis
1. AI-Powered Climate Forecasting
Machine learning models combine atmospheric, oceanic, and land data to

simulate future climate scenarios with precision. Governments use these forecasts to shape resilient infrastructure and emergency policies.

2. Smart Energy Optimization

AI manages renewable grids in real time, forecasting solar radiation, wind strength, and energy demand. It reduces reliance on fossil fuels while keeping lights on in every home.

3. Carbon Capture and Storage Efficiency

AI analyzes geological data to locate ideal sites for carbon storage and monitors the long-term safety of underground reservoirs. It also optimizes industrial carbon capture systems to maximize output.

4. Disaster Response and Recovery Systems

During crises, AI assists emergency coordinators by mapping evacuation routes, analyzing social media distress signals, and deploying autonomous drones for search and rescue. Recovery becomes faster and more organized.

5. Precision Agriculture

AI guides irrigation systems, fertilization, and pest control — using just the right resources at the right time. This not only boosts yield but reduces pollution and water waste.

6. Circular Economy and Waste Reduction

AI platforms identify recyclable materials, predict waste trends, and manage supply chains to minimize environmental footprint. Manufacturing becomes sustainable by design, not by afterthought.

7. Ocean and Air Quality Monitoring

Autonomous AI buoys and drones continuously monitor pollution levels and ecosystem changes, providing live feedback to scientists and policy makers.

The Effects on Business and Policy

Green Investment Acceleration: AI-driven analytics highlight profitable sustainability projects, pushing investors toward green technologies and renewable ventures.

AI-Verified Carbon Credits: Smart contracts ensure the authenticity of carbon trading, eliminating fraud and increasing trust in global markets.

Environmental Policy Enforcement: Governments use AI surveillance systems to enforce emissions laws and track illegal logging, mining, or overfishing in near-real time.

Human and Ethical Considerations

While AI offers incredible power in environmental management, it also raises moral questions: Who controls climate data? Who decides which regions receive intervention first? These issues have inspired new "Eco-Ethics Councils" — human oversight boards ensuring fairness, accountability, and transparency in AI-led environmental programs.

The guiding principle: AI must serve the planet, not politics.

The Planet's Smartest Ally

Climate Intelligence Systems have given Earth a digital nervous system — one capable of feeling, analyzing, and responding to threats faster than ever. But the ultimate goal of 2026

isn't to let machines save the planet; it's to help humanity learn how to live intelligently within it.
AI doesn't just measure sustainability — it teaches it.
And in doing so, it transforms the greatest challenge of our time into a shared mission of innovation, empathy, and hope.

Chapter 10 – Autonomous Transportation Breakthrough

The Road to Self-Thinking Mobility

By 2026, the phrase "self-driving" no longer sounds futuristic — it's part of daily life. Artificial Intelligence now powers a worldwide network of autonomous cars, drones, ships, and delivery robots. Streets hum with coordination instead of chaos, and the old frustrations of commuting — traffic jams, road rage, human error — are fading into history.

The global transportation system has undergone its greatest transformation since the invention of the automobile. AI doesn't simply move machines; it moves entire societies toward efficiency, safety, and sustainability.

Reasons Behind the Autonomous Transportation Revolution

1. Technological Maturity of AI Vision Systems

Machine vision and sensor fusion technologies — combining cameras, LiDAR, radar, and GPS — have reached near-human perception accuracy. Vehicles can recognize objects, gestures, and hazards in milliseconds, even in poor weather or at night.

2. Advancements in Edge Computing and Connectivity

Real-time decision making now happens locally within each vehicle. Combined with ultra-fast 6G networks, cars, trucks, and drones share situational data instantly, forming a collective intelligence that prevents accidents and optimizes flow.

3. Human Error and Safety Demands

Ninety percent of historical road accidents stemmed from human mistakes. With the rise of urban congestion and distracted driving, societies demanded safer systems. AI offered not just automation, but judgment — rapid, bias-free decisions grounded in data.

4. Environmental Imperative

As nations pursued net-zero goals, autonomous electric fleets emerged as a dual solution: reducing emissions and optimizing energy consumption. AI manages routes for maximum efficiency, conserving both time and fuel.

5. Economic Efficiency and Workforce Evolution

Logistics, shipping, and ride-sharing companies faced rising labor shortages and costs. AI-driven fleets reduced downtime and increased delivery precision, creating new categories of work in maintenance, supervision, and fleet analytics.

6. Policy and Infrastructure Alignment

Governments finally caught up. Unified traffic data systems and "smart infrastructure" — roads embedded with sensors, AI traffic lights, and connected intersections — made wide-scale autonomy feasible.

The Effects on Daily Life and Global Systems

1. Dramatic Reduction in Accidents and Fatalities

Accident rates have dropped by over 80% in cities with fully autonomous fleets. AI's ability to predict collisions, maintain safe distances, and communicate between vehicles has nearly eliminated common traffic errors.

2. End of Congestion and Idle Time

AI coordinates urban traffic dynamically. It reroutes vehicles based on weather, density, and emergency conditions, minimizing idle time and cutting commute hours significantly.

3. Transformation of Urban Design

With self-parking and shared vehicle models, cities reclaimed space once devoted to parking lots and gas stations. Green zones, walking paths, and community gardens now occupy former asphalt deserts.

4. Accessibility for All

The elderly, visually impaired, and physically challenged now enjoy unprecedented independence. AI-guided vehicles provide affordable, on-demand mobility without the need for human drivers.

5. Economic Realignment

New industries have risen around data management, AI maintenance, battery recycling, and transportation analytics. Traditional driving jobs have evolved into oversight, programming, and service supervision roles.

6. Public Trust and Ethical Challenges

Society's confidence in AI transportation grew through transparency — open data policies, public testing, and real-time safety reporting. Still, debates persist about liability in rare cases of system failure, prompting ongoing legal innovation.

How AI Provides Solutions in Transportation

1. Predictive Navigation Systems
AI integrates satellite data, road sensors, and traffic feeds to forecast congestion hours in advance. Vehicles reroute automatically, ensuring optimal travel times and lower emissions.

2. Fleet Coordination and Logistics Management
Global shipping and delivery rely on AI orchestration that manages fleets of autonomous trucks, ships, and drones. Algorithms calculate the most efficient distribution routes, cutting delivery costs and fuel waste.

3. AI-Managed Public Transit
City buses, trams, and metro systems operate through AI scheduling, ensuring vehicles arrive precisely when demand peaks. Public transport becomes faster, more reliable, and safer for passengers.

4. Emergency Response Integration
Autonomous ambulances and drones coordinate with hospitals, transmitting patient vitals en route. Police and fire departments deploy AI vehicles for rapid, route-optimized interventions.

5. Sustainable Energy Optimization
Electric autonomous vehicles communicate directly with smart grids, charging during off-peak hours and feeding stored power back into the grid when demand spikes.

6. Aerial Mobility and Drone Delivery
AI flight systems manage low-altitude airways for drones transporting goods, medical

supplies, and emergency kits. Cities use 3D air-traffic mapping to prevent collisions and noise pollution.

7. Maritime and Freight Autonomy

Cargo ships now use AI navigation to optimize fuel use, adjust for weather, and reduce emissions. Ports employ robotic loading systems that synchronize with vessel AI for near-zero downtime.

8. Ethical AI Driving Frameworks

Moral reasoning models govern autonomous decisions during split-second emergencies, ensuring that safety, legality, and fairness guide every outcome.

The Environmental and Social Impact

AI's orchestration of electric and hybrid fleets has drastically cut greenhouse emissions in the transportation sector. Freight industries once responsible for 20% of CO_2 output now operate with measurable sustainability goals. Beyond environmental benefits, accessibility has expanded opportunities: students in rural areas can travel to schools; patients reach hospitals on time; deliveries arrive even in storm conditions. Transportation is no longer a privilege of mobility but a right of connection.

The Human-AI Partnership on the Move

Humans still play a vital role — as supervisors, designers, ethicists, and engineers. Pilots, captains, and drivers haven't disappeared; they've evolved into system monitors who guide fleets with wisdom AI can't replicate: empathy, ethics, and experience.

The great lesson of the autonomous revolution is that progress doesn't remove people — it redefines them. Where once we sat behind the wheel, we now sit at the helm of innovation.

A World That Moves Itself
In 2026, roads are safer, skies are smarter, and cities breathe easier. Artificial Intelligence has turned transportation into an intelligent network of motion — predictive, responsive, and self-healing.
The breakthrough of autonomy isn't just about moving vehicles — it's about moving civilization forward.
AI doesn't just take us places faster.
It takes us to a better future.

Chapter 11 – Smart Cities and Digital Governance

The City That Thinks for Itself

By 2026, the world's great cities have come alive — not metaphorically, but literally. Networks of sensors, data streams, and Artificial Intelligence systems hum beneath the streets and across skylines, managing everything from traffic lights to public health alerts. The "smart city" has evolved from a futuristic concept into a functioning organism: self-aware, self-correcting, and citizen-centered.

Artificial Intelligence is the brain of these cities, processing billions of inputs each second to keep urban life efficient, safe, and sustainable. This is not about replacing government — it's about enhancing governance through real-time insight and collective intelligence.

Reasons Behind the Rise of Smart Cities

1. Exploding Urban Populations

Over two-thirds of humanity now lives in cities. Managing resources, transportation, waste, and infrastructure at that scale required automation far beyond human capability. AI emerged as the central nervous system that keeps the urban organism alive.

2. Technological Maturity and Data Connectivity

The global adoption of 6G networks, IoT devices, and edge computing enables instant communication between machines, infrastructure, and citizens. Cities can now "listen" to themselves — detecting problems before humans even notice them.

3. Demand for Sustainable Urban Living
Climate goals, pollution control, and energy optimization became urgent priorities. Governments turned to AI to monitor environmental data, regulate consumption, and transition to greener infrastructure.

4. Administrative Overload and Inefficiency
Bureaucratic bottlenecks and human error slowed traditional governance. AI stepped in to handle the data-heavy work: processing permits, predicting maintenance, and optimizing public services.

5. Rise of Digital Citizenship
Citizens now expect transparency, instant access, and participation. AI-driven platforms provide digital town halls, real-time updates, and equitable service distribution across communities.

The Effects of AI-Driven Urban Systems

1. Hyper-Efficient Infrastructure
AI manages water systems, electricity grids, and public transit in real time. Smart grids reduce power waste by predicting peak hours, while AI monitors detect pipe leaks or structural stress before damage occurs.

2. Traffic-Free Mobility
AI-coordinated traffic lights and autonomous vehicles communicate directly with city infrastructure. Commute times in major smart cities have dropped by up to 40%. Emergency vehicles receive "green light corridors," ensuring zero-delay response.

3. Environmental Monitoring and Response

Urban AI systems track air quality, waste output, and temperature changes, triggering automatic interventions. Drones clean polluted waterways; smart bins sort recyclables; and rooftop sensors adjust building emissions dynamically.

4. Improved Public Safety

AI-powered surveillance and predictive policing tools identify unusual behavior or potential hazards while maintaining strong privacy safeguards. Fire and rescue systems use predictive mapping to anticipate high-risk zones before disasters strike.

5. Participatory Digital Governance

Citizens interact directly with government AI portals. From submitting feedback to voting on local issues, residents experience transparent democracy enhanced by digital engagement and blockchain-based verification.

6. Economic and Energy Efficiency

AI predicts economic fluctuations within city economies and adjusts taxation, subsidies, and incentives dynamically. Smart buildings adjust energy use autonomously, cutting costs for both cities and citizens.

How AI Provides Solutions in Smart Cities

1. Urban Planning and Simulation

AI-driven "digital twins" — virtual replicas of entire cities — simulate the effects of new policies, infrastructure changes, or population growth before they're implemented. This prevents costly mistakes and improves long-term sustainability.

2. Resource Distribution and Waste Reduction

Algorithms analyze population data to allocate resources precisely where needed — from emergency supplies to education funding — ensuring equity across neighborhoods.

3. Predictive Maintenance Systems

AI monitors bridges, roads, and utility lines for micro-cracks, vibrations, or irregularities. Predictive alerts prevent breakdowns before they happen, saving billions in repair costs and avoiding human injury.

4. Smart Governance Platforms

Administrative processes like licensing, permits, and citizen support are automated through chatbots and natural language systems. Residents can renew documents, report issues, or access benefits instantly.

5. Disaster Preparedness and Response

AI integrates meteorological and structural data to forecast natural disasters. Cities use drone fleets and autonomous rescue vehicles to coordinate evacuation and resource delivery safely and swiftly.

6. Transparent Budgeting and Policy Simulation

AI analyzes spending patterns and public impact. City leaders can simulate how different budget allocations affect health, housing, or transportation outcomes — empowering evidence-based decision-making.

7. Cybersecurity and Data Privacy

With so much urban data at stake, AI also guards its own infrastructure. Machine learning models detect and neutralize cyberattacks on traffic systems, utilities, and financial networks before they escalate.

8. AI for Public Health Management

City health dashboards track disease patterns, vaccination rates, and hospital capacity. AI models predict outbreaks early and allocate resources accordingly, protecting millions of lives.

The Human Experience of Living in Smart Cities

Life in AI-powered cities feels intuitive. Streetlights dim or brighten as people walk by. Buses arrive exactly when needed. Garbage bins send alerts before overflowing. Even weather forecasting integrates with personal schedules — suggesting when to leave home or bike instead of drive.

Yet amid all this automation, the most successful cities maintain a human pulse. Digital governance does not replace empathy; it amplifies it. Public feedback, ethical oversight, and cultural inclusion ensure that AI-driven progress benefits everyone, not just the wealthy or tech-savvy.

The Balance of Power and Responsibility

With great intelligence comes great accountability. In 2026, debates continue over how far AI should go in decision-making. Can a machine approve a building permit? Enforce a fine? Prioritize one neighborhood's repair over another's?

To resolve this, governments have introduced AI Oversight Councils — diverse panels of citizens, ethicists, and engineers who evaluate algorithms and ensure human judgment remains at the heart of public life.

The City as a Living Network

Smart Cities in 2026 represent humanity's attempt to synchronize progress with compassion. Artificial Intelligence doesn't just optimize systems — it reconnects them. Each traffic light, water pipe, and city sensor contributes to a unified ecosystem designed for balance.

These cities are no longer static structures; they're living networks that grow and learn. AI listens. It adapts. It evolves alongside its citizens.

And for the first time in history, the city itself is not just a place where people live —
it's a partner in how they live.

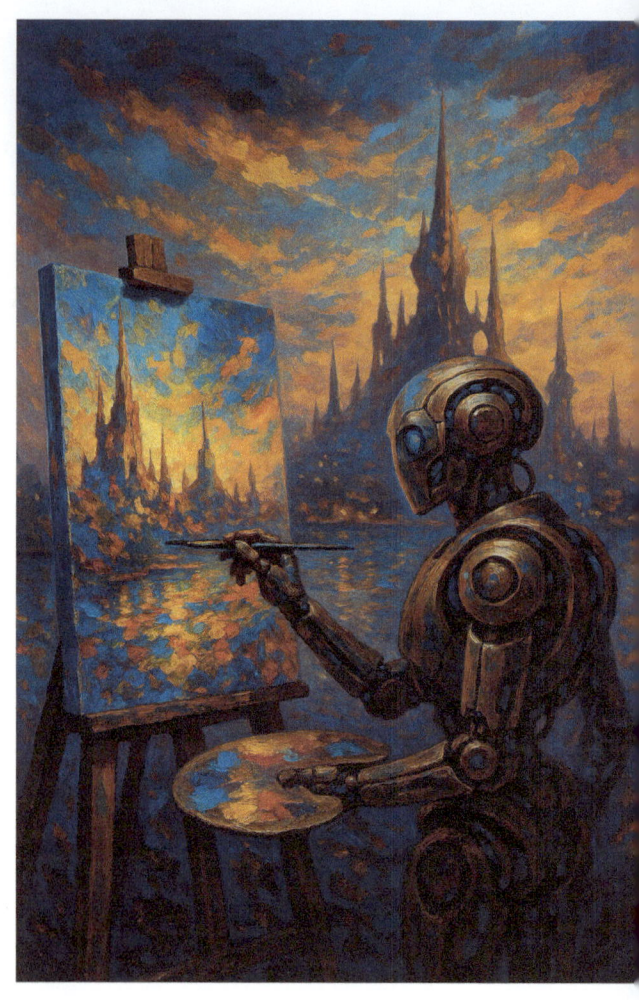

Chapter 12 – The Great AI Art Renaissance

When Machines Learn to Imagine

By 2026, the boundary between artist and algorithm has dissolved.
Artificial Intelligence has become a creative collaborator — painting, composing, writing, designing, and sculpting alongside humans. The world is experiencing a new kind of renaissance: not one defined by brushes and marble, but by data, pattern, and imagination. AI doesn't dream in the same way humans do, yet its interpretations of color, form, and emotion have expanded the very meaning of creativity. What began as experimental generative art in the early 2020s has matured into a flourishing movement where humanity's oldest instinct — to express — now meets its newest invention — to compute.

Reasons Behind the AI Art Renaissance

1. Democratization of Creative Tools
Powerful AI art and design systems have become accessible to everyone, not just professionals. Anyone with an idea can create polished visual, musical, or written art in seconds, unlocking creative expression for millions who never saw themselves as artists.

2. Generative Model Breakthroughs
Advances in multimodal AI — capable of combining image, text, sound, and motion — allow for the seamless creation of complex, multidimensional works. Artists can now "converse" with AI to refine visual tone,

emotional depth, and narrative meaning.

3. Integration Across Creative Industries

Film studios, architects, advertisers, and fashion designers now rely on AI to generate concepts, predict trends, and personalize experiences. This synergy has accelerated innovation while reducing production costs and time.

4. Cultural Desire for Authentic Innovation

After decades of digital saturation, society craved authenticity and imagination. Ironically, AI became the tool that reawakened creativity by making artistic exploration faster, freer, and more intuitive.

5. Rise of Creator Economies and NFTs

Blockchain technologies allowed artists to protect, sell, and track digital art. AI integration further empowered creators to produce, distribute, and monetize their work without corporate gatekeepers.

The Effects of AI on Global Creativity

1. Explosion of Global Participation

AI has given voice to billions who lacked access to art education or tools. From rural communities to urban centers, people are creating music, design, and stories — contributing to the most diverse creative landscape in history.

2. Rebirth of Collaboration

Artists now partner with AI systems as they once did with fellow humans. A poet guides an AI that paints. A musician composes with an AI that visualizes melodies. Every project becomes a dialogue between imagination and intelligence.

3. Transformation of Art Education

Schools now use AI to teach composition, color theory, and storytelling. Students explore artistic principles interactively, guided by virtual mentors that adapt lessons to each learner's style and pace.

4. New Aesthetic Movements

A distinct "AI aesthetic" has emerged — blending human imperfection with machine precision. Styles like Neural Impressionism and Algorithmic Surrealism dominate galleries, museums, and digital showcases.

5. Cultural and Ethical Debate

Critics question authorship and originality: Who is the artist — the human who prompts or the AI that produces? Philosophers argue that creativity is not just in output but in intention — and since humans still direct the creative process, art remains deeply human.

6. Industry Evolution and Economic Expansion

The creative economy has exploded. AI allows small creators to produce high-quality work at scale, lowering barriers to entry and creating new industries in interactive storytelling, immersive design, and generative music.

How AI Provides Solutions in the Creative World

1. Creative Amplification

AI tools help artists break creative blocks by suggesting variations, color palettes, melodies, or story continuations. The result isn't automation — it's augmentation of imagination.

2. Cultural Preservation

AI archives, reconstructs, and revives ancient art forms. Lost manuscripts, damaged frescoes, and extinct languages are digitally restored, ensuring cultural heritage is never lost to time.

3. Personalized Artistic Experiences

Museums and virtual galleries use AI to tailor experiences to each visitor's taste. Viewers see customized exhibitions, hear personalized soundscapes, and even interact with living artworks that respond to mood and movement.

4. Inclusive Creation Platforms

For people with disabilities, AI enables new artistic access. Voice-to-paint, gesture-controlled music synthesis, and neural-guided sketching empower all users to create beyond physical limits.

5. Sustainable Art Production

AI reduces material waste by simulating designs before physical creation. Architects test concepts digitally. Fashion designers model entire collections virtually, saving energy, fabric, and emissions.

6. Cross-Disciplinary Innovation

AI acts as a bridge between art and science. Environmental data becomes sculpture, mathematics becomes melody, and human emotion becomes visual form. Creativity becomes not just an art — but an ecosystem.

7. Emotional Resonance Modeling

New AI systems interpret emotion in art — adjusting lighting, tone, or sound to evoke specific feelings. Creators use this to heighten empathy, making art a more immersive human experience.

The Effects on Artists and Society

Artists once afraid of being replaced have discovered something profound: AI doesn't steal creativity — it magnifies it. The best creators of 2026 are directors of possibility, guiding intelligent systems to explore beyond human limitations.

A sculptor can now test infinite materials before touching clay.

A musician can hear a symphony performed by an orchestra that doesn't exist.

A writer can see their world visualized in motion and sound.

The creative process becomes faster, more emotional, and more connected than ever before.

Ethics, Ownership, and the New Creative Contract

The AI Art Renaissance also forces a redefinition of ownership and authenticity. Legislators and artists have collaborated on AI Authorship Standards, ensuring that creators retain rights over any artwork they generate, direct, or inspire.

AI developers, meanwhile, are required to disclose data sources used in training, preventing cultural plagiarism or bias in generated art. The principle is simple: the artist leads, the algorithm follows.

A Future Painted by Two Hands

In this new Renaissance, creativity is not about replacing one artist with another — it's about fusing imagination across species. Human

intuition meets digital precision. Passion meets pattern.
Art in 2026 is no longer defined by what the hand can make, but by what the mind can imagine.
And as AI joins that imagination, it becomes clear that technology's greatest masterpiece isn't the art it creates — it's the creativity it inspires.

Chapter 13 – Voice as the New Keyboard

When Words Become the Interface

By 2026, humanity has returned to its oldest form of communication — the spoken word — but in a radically new way. Artificial Intelligence has turned voice into the universal interface for the digital world.
No longer do people type, swipe, or click to interact with technology. They speak. From commanding household robots to composing books, managing businesses, and translating conversations in real time, AI understands speech with the precision of language itself. The world is entering the era of frictionless interaction, where technology listens, learns, and responds — naturally, intuitively, and conversationally.

Reasons Behind the Voice Revolution
1. Advancements in Natural Language Processing (NLP)
AI models have achieved human-like fluency in understanding speech, tone, and context. By 2026, even regional dialects, slang, and emotional inflection are accurately interpreted — eliminating the awkward misunderstandings of early voice assistants.
2. Integration of Voice with Everyday Devices
From cars and appliances to workplace tools and wearable tech, voice interfaces are now standard. The ability to control, inquire, and create using natural speech has made technology accessible to everyone — regardless of literacy or physical ability.

3. Multilingual Mastery

Real-time translation models allow seamless cross-language conversation. Whether a meeting involves people speaking English, Spanish, or Mandarin, AI translates instantly and smoothly, bridging cultural divides.

4. Hands-Free Efficiency in a Mobile World

As remote work and multitasking continue to dominate, users needed faster, safer, and more flexible ways to interact. Voice-based systems free people from screens, enabling communication on the go.

5. Human Desire for Connection and Personality in Technology

Users prefer talking to an empathetic, responsive AI over typing commands into a machine. Designers responded by making AI voices expressive, human-like, and emotionally intelligent.

The Effects of Voice-First AI on Society

1. Universal Accessibility

Voice technology empowers millions who once struggled with reading, vision impairments, or typing. Seniors, children, and people with disabilities can now access information and communicate effortlessly.

2. A Shift in Human-Computer Relationship

Talking to machines is no longer odd — it's natural. Families discuss recipes with their kitchen assistants; workers verbally organize schedules; writers dictate novels to AI co-authors. The human-machine barrier dissolves into conversation.

3. Cultural Preservation Through Language

AI systems have learned thousands of dialects

and endangered languages. By embedding voice data into translation and storytelling tools, ancient tongues are preserved and revitalized through daily digital use.

4. Business and Customer Experience Transformation

Companies now operate conversational AI support systems that understand nuance, intent, and emotion. Instead of menus or chatbots, customers have smooth, empathetic voice interactions 24/7.

5. Privacy and Trust Challenges

As always, innovation brings new dilemmas. Voice data is sensitive — revealing identity, mood, and even location. Ethical voice design and encrypted AI processing ensure security and transparency in how voice information is used.

6. Voice-Driven Creativity

Artists, musicians, and content creators use speech to compose, direct, and produce.
A simple conversation with an AI can generate visual art, soundscapes, or narrative experiences in minutes.

How AI Provides Solutions in a Voice-Driven World

1. Contextual Understanding and Memory

AI doesn't just hear words — it understands meaning. Systems remember user preferences, previous conversations, and emotional states to offer personalized responses and continuity in dialogue.

2. Real-Time Translation and Transcription

Multilingual meetings and classrooms benefit from instant, accurate transcription. AI listens to multiple speakers simultaneously, identifies each voice, and delivers live captions or translations for every participant.

3. Voice-Powered Productivity Tools

In workplaces, employees dictate reports, code snippets, or creative briefs. AI summarizes, edits, and formats automatically, turning spoken ideas into publish-ready documents.

4. Smart Homes and Cities Controlled by Speech

Lighting, temperature, and transportation can be adjusted through simple conversation. Public infrastructure integrates voice access points, allowing citizens to report issues or request information instantly.

5. Healthcare and Emergency Services

Doctors use voice commands during procedures, nurses record patient data verbally, and elderly users call for help simply by speaking. AI listens for distress signals and alerts responders automatically.

6. Education and Learning Enhancement

Students now interact verbally with AI tutors. They ask questions, discuss topics, and practice languages through natural conversation. AI adjusts tone and vocabulary to suit each learner's age and comprehension level.

7. Personal Companions and Emotional Wellness

Emotional AI voice systems offer empathy-driven conversation. They detect loneliness, anxiety, or stress in tone and respond with care, mindfulness exercises, or supportive dialogue — redefining digital companionship.

8. Creative Expression Through Voice-to-Art

Storytellers and musicians use "voice sketching" — describing scenes, moods, or rhythms — which AI transforms into visual compositions or symphonies. Spoken imagination becomes art.

The Economic and Cultural Ripple Effects
Voice commerce (V-commerce) has emerged as a dominant trend. People shop by speaking, negotiate contracts verbally, and control finances using voice-verified authentication. Media consumption, marketing, and entertainment now revolve around conversational engagement instead of screens. Culturally, voice-driven systems are reviving oral traditions — storytelling, poetry, and community dialogue — giving humanity's oldest art form a digital stage.

Ethical Framework and Human Oversight
The 2026 voice revolution also brings responsibility. Governments and developers have implemented Voice Ethics Protocols requiring user consent for recordings and transparency in AI voice generation. Deepfake voice replication — once a major threat — is now traceable through secure watermarking. These ethical safeguards ensure that technology amplifies truth, not deception.

A World That Speaks Back
The rise of voice-based AI has humanized technology. Where once we clicked, now we converse. Where once we scrolled, now we speak — and technology answers in kind. The most profound change isn't in how we

communicate with machines — it's how they listen to us.
In this new age, every voice matters, every language counts, and every conversation builds a bridge between people and possibility. AI has made the world not just more connected, but more heard.

Chapter 14 – Quantum Meets Artificial Intelligence

The Fusion of Two Revolutions

By 2026, two of the most transformative forces in human history — Artificial Intelligence and Quantum Computing — have begun to merge. Their convergence marks the beginning of what scientists call the Quantum-AI Era — an age where machines can think, learn, and simulate at scales previously impossible. Quantum computing provides AI with something traditional computers could never offer: true exponential power. In return, AI provides quantum systems with the structure, optimization, and adaptability they need to function meaningfully. Together, they have broken the limits of speed, complexity, and imagination.

Reasons Behind the Quantum-AI Convergence

1. Limitations of Classical Computing

Traditional processors, no matter how fast, hit bottlenecks when modeling complex systems such as climate prediction, protein folding, or global economies. Quantum computing, using qubits instead of bits, can process multiple possibilities simultaneously — something AI desperately needed to handle vast real-world data.

2. Breakthroughs in Quantum Hardware Stability

Quantum computers in 2026 are far more stable and accessible than their fragile prototypes of the early 2020s. Error correction, cryogenic efficiency, and photonic qubits have made quantum systems practical for commercial and scientific use.

3. AI-Driven Quantum Optimization
Artificial Intelligence plays a critical role in controlling quantum systems, fine-tuning parameters, and reducing error rates. In essence, AI makes quantum computing operationally intelligent.

4. Global Demand for Faster Problem Solving
As data and challenges exploded in scale — from financial forecasting to genetic research — society required new forms of computation that could simulate and solve with unprecedented speed and accuracy.

5. Government and Private Investment
Leading nations and tech giants have made enormous investments in quantum-AI research partnerships. This collaboration between science, policy, and enterprise has accelerated innovation and created a race for quantum supremacy — ethically guided by shared global standards.

The Effects of Quantum-AI Integration
1. A Leap in Computational Power
Quantum-AI hybrids process information millions of times faster than classical systems. Tasks that once required weeks — like training a massive AI model or decoding genomic data — can now be completed in seconds.

2. Breakthroughs in Scientific Discovery
Drug discovery, materials science, and energy research have exploded with innovation. AI-powered quantum simulations allow scientists

to test millions of molecular combinations virtually, leading to cleaner energy, advanced medicine, and sustainable materials.

3. Unprecedented Accuracy in Predictions
From weather forecasting to financial risk modeling, predictive AI now runs on quantum engines that analyze probabilities across multiple realities simultaneously. Forecasts that once carried uncertainty now approach near-perfect precision.

4. Economic and Competitive Shifts
The nations and companies that first harnessed quantum-AI gained enormous economic and strategic advantages, transforming the global balance of power. However, cooperative research initiatives have helped ensure that breakthroughs benefit humanity rather than create inequality.

5. New Forms of Creativity and Art
Artists and engineers now use quantum-powered AI to visualize higher-dimensional art, compose symphonies of infinite variation, and design structures inspired by physics itself — where imagination meets mathematics.

6. Ethical and Security Challenges
Quantum-AI power also introduces new risks: potential decryption of global data, manipulation of digital markets, and the creation of "black box" intelligences too complex for even their creators to fully understand.

How AI and Quantum Together Provide Solutions
1. Solving the Unsolvable
Quantum-enhanced AI models can solve

optimization problems that were once computationally impossible — such as mapping the global supply chain for zero waste or designing perfect renewable energy systems.

2. Accelerating Medical Research
Quantum-AI simulations model protein folding and disease behavior with atomic-level accuracy. Lifesaving treatments for cancer, Alzheimer's, and genetic disorders are discovered faster than ever before.

3. Climate Modeling and Sustainability
AI interprets planetary-scale climate data through quantum simulations, forecasting decades ahead with unprecedented resolution. Governments use this information to plan infrastructure and reduce emissions intelligently.

4. Cybersecurity Reinvention
Paradoxically, while quantum computing can crack current encryption, it also powers quantum-secure algorithms that safeguard data through principles of entanglement and uncertainty — creating an unbreakable digital shield.

5. Financial and Economic Optimization
Quantum AI can simulate entire economies, identifying the smallest inefficiencies in markets, logistics, and global trade. Banks and governments use it to stabilize inflation, reduce risk, and design fairer systems of exchange.

6. Autonomous Scientific Research
AI scientists, running on quantum platforms, autonomously design experiments, test hypotheses, and iterate results — speeding up

global innovation cycles tenfold.

7. Ethical Oversight Systems
AI-powered ethics monitors, built into quantum systems, ensure that research and applications stay within moral and regulatory frameworks. These embedded safeguards provide accountability in an otherwise limitless realm of computation.

The Societal Transformation
The Quantum-AI era has accelerated humanity's collective intelligence. Education systems now train "quantum thinkers" — individuals fluent in probability, logic, and empathy. Universities collaborate globally through shared quantum networks that simulate social and ecological solutions in real time.
For the first time, human knowledge and machine learning evolve together, interlinked by a computational system capable of processing not just information, but understanding.

The Human Role in a Quantum World
Though quantum machines operate beyond human comprehension, humans remain their architects and conscience. Scientists emphasize interpretability — designing systems that can explain decisions in ways humans can follow.
This partnership ensures that progress remains guided by values, not just velocity. The frontier of intelligence is no longer about creating machines that think like humans — but machines that help humans think beyond

what was ever possible.

A Universe of Infinite Possibility

The union of quantum computing and Artificial Intelligence is more than a technological milestone — it is a philosophical one. It forces humanity to reconsider the limits of reason, imagination, and even reality itself.
AI gave us pattern.
Quantum computing gave us probability.
Together, they've given us potential without boundaries.
In the quantum age, we no longer ask what machines can do — we ask what humanity can become when we collaborate with them.
The future is not just faster — it's infinitely smarter.

Chapter 15 – The Future of Jobs and Reskilling

A World Redefined by Intelligence

By 2026, Artificial Intelligence has become both the world's most powerful coworker and its greatest disruptor. Nearly every profession — from manufacturing and marketing to healthcare and design — has been touched by automation, analytics, and machine learning. But instead of destroying work, AI is transforming it.

The age of mass redundancy has given way to an age of mass reinvention. Humans are not being replaced; they are being redefined — learning to focus on creativity, empathy, and leadership while machines handle precision, repetition, and data.

The result is a global shift toward lifelong learning, fluid career paths, and a reimagined partnership between human ingenuity and digital intelligence.

Reasons Behind the Workforce Transformation

1. Automation of Routine Work

From data entry to scheduling, machines now complete millions of tasks once handled by humans. This automation has freed workers to focus on roles requiring strategic thinking, emotion, and innovation.

2. Acceleration of Digital Transformation

The pandemic years of the early 2020s forced companies to digitize rapidly. By 2026, remote collaboration, virtual operations, and intelligent analytics are the foundation of business, demanding new skill sets in every industry.

3. Emergence of Hybrid Human-AI Teams

The workforce is no longer divided between people and machines — it's a collaboration. Humans provide creativity, ethical judgment, and storytelling; AI provides speed, precision, and scalability.

4. Demographic and Global Shifts

As populations age and industries evolve, AI fills critical labor shortages in healthcare, logistics, and education. At the same time, it opens new opportunities for youth in data, robotics, and digital craftsmanship.

5. Demand for Adaptability and Continuous Learning

The half-life of skills has dropped below five years. Workers must constantly re-learn and adapt to new technologies, creating a culture where education no longer ends with graduation — it evolves with the individual.

6. Corporate and Government Investment in Reskilling

Recognizing the scale of disruption, organizations and nations now prioritize workforce retraining programs. AI itself designs and manages these programs, customizing them to personal abilities and learning styles.

The Effects of AI on the Global Workforce

1. Creation of New Job Categories

AI has birthed professions that didn't exist a decade ago: Algorithm Ethicists, AI Trainers, Data Storytellers, Human-AI Experience

Designers, and Digital Wellbeing Coaches. These roles blend technical literacy with creativity and empathy.

2. Decline of Traditional Employment Models

Permanent positions are giving way to flexible, project-based work. AI platforms match talent with demand instantly, forming "liquid workforces" where teams assemble dynamically for specific goals.

3. Rise of Human-Centered Skills

As automation handles the technical, human success depends on emotional intelligence, adaptability, collaboration, and ethical reasoning. The future belongs to those who know how to lead and communicate — not just calculate.

4. Global Reskilling Renaissance

Education has become modular, mobile, and AI-driven. Individuals build skills through microlearning courses and virtual apprenticeships guided by intelligent tutors. This democratizes opportunity, empowering people in both urban centers and rural villages.

5. Reduction in Work Stress and Burnout

Intelligent automation reduces administrative load. AI wellness assistants monitor workloads and recommend breaks, ensuring balance between productivity and health. Companies find that happy employees are now their greatest advantage.

6. Ethical Questions and Workforce Equity

Some worry about inequality — that automation benefits the skilled while excluding those without digital access. In response, governments and NGOs deploy AI tools specifically for inclusion, providing free education, translation, and skill guidance to the underserved.

How AI Provides Solutions for the Future of Work

1. Personalized Learning and Career Guidance
AI analyzes a person's strengths, interests, and performance history to create individualized learning paths. It identifies market needs and matches workers with emerging roles that fit their potential.

2. AI-Powered Reskilling Platforms
Intelligent learning systems — used by major corporations and governments — design adaptive training programs that evolve in real time. Workers no longer study static curricula; they learn what's relevant today.

3. Talent Matching and Employment Forecasting
Machine learning models predict which industries will grow, which roles will decline, and what skills will be in demand. Job seekers and students use these insights to make informed career choices before change happens.

4. Inclusive Access and Language Adaptation
AI translation and voice learning allow people in any region to learn in their native language. Barriers of geography, language, and disability are being erased by intelligent access design.

5. Corporate AI Mentors and Coaches
Digital career assistants guide employees through new technologies, provide instant support, and track long-term development. This fosters loyalty, engagement, and

confidence in workplaces navigating constant change.

6. Automation of Menial Workflows
By eliminating repetitive tasks — such as form processing, data migration, and compliance reporting — AI allows professionals to focus on innovation and human connection, leading to higher satisfaction and better results.

7. Workforce Analytics and Predictive HR
AI analyzes organizational data to identify performance trends, prevent burnout, and ensure fair evaluation. It recommends promotions, team restructuring, and diversity initiatives based on merit and behavioral insight.

8. AI-Driven Apprenticeships
Digital apprenticeship programs pair learners with virtual mentors in their chosen industries. These AI mentors track progress, provide feedback, and simulate real-world scenarios for immersive training.

Cultural and Economic Effects

1. The Learning Economy Emerges
Education is now the world's fastest-growing industry. Continuous reskilling has become a social norm, with governments offering "learning credits" and AI universities providing tailored credentials on demand.

2. Revaluation of Work Itself
Success is no longer measured solely by job titles or income but by contribution, creativity, and lifelong growth. The workplace becomes a platform for purpose as much as profit.

3. Flattened Corporate Structures
With AI managing data and reporting,

traditional hierarchies dissolve. Decision-making becomes collaborative and transparent. Every worker has access to the same insights, creating more democratic organizations.

4. Work-Life Synergy

Flexible hours, remote collaboration, and smart wellness tools foster equilibrium between personal and professional life. AI ensures efficiency without erasing humanity.

The Human Role in an Automated Economy
In the AI-driven economy, humans are no longer defined by repetition but by reinvention.

Every job becomes a dialogue between human insight and machine intelligence. The most successful workers are not those who resist automation but those who guide it — shaping systems that reflect human values and creativity.

As machines learn to work like us, we must learn to think like inventors, dreamers, and philosophers once more. The skills of the future are empathy, ethics, adaptability, and storytelling — timeless abilities that no algorithm can replicate.

A Workforce Reborn
The future of work is not about survival — it's about evolution.
AI has not ended employment; it has ended monotony.
It has not stolen purpose; it has given us new reasons to learn, to grow, and to lead.
In 2026, the greatest skill is no longer knowing

how to do one thing well — but how to keep learning in a world that never stops changing. AI doesn't just automate tasks; it awakens talent.
And in that awakening, humanity rediscovers the true meaning of work — creation, contribution, and continuous becoming.

Chapter 16 – Security in the Age of Algorithms

When Intelligence Becomes the First Line of Defense

By 2026, the battlefield for security — personal, corporate, and national — has shifted almost entirely into the digital realm. Firewalls and passwords are relics of the past. Today, Artificial Intelligence defends the world in real time, scanning, predicting, and neutralizing threats faster than any human team ever could.

The age of algorithms is both empowering and perilous. The same intelligence that protects hospitals, banks, and governments also arms hackers, scammers, and cyberwarriors. Humanity's challenge is no longer whether it can secure data — but whether it can outthink its own machines.

Reasons Behind the Rise of AI-Powered Security

1. Explosion of Data and Connectivity
By 2026, nearly every object — from refrigerators to city grids — is connected to the internet. This "Internet of Everything" produces massive vulnerability surfaces. Only AI systems can monitor and defend this scale of interconnection.

2. Surge in Cyber Threat Sophistication
Attacks are now autonomous. Malware learns, adapts, and evolves using AI — capable of rewriting itself to bypass traditional defenses.

Human analysts alone can't keep up with threats that mutate by the second.

3. Growth of Cloud and Decentralized Infrastructure

As businesses moved operations online, data scattered across thousands of servers and networks. AI's distributed intelligence now acts as the glue that identifies threats and enforces security across this vast digital terrain.

4. Rise of Deepfakes and Misinformation

AI-generated content has blurred the line between truth and deception. Governments, media, and corporations turned to counter-AI systems to detect manipulation and preserve authenticity.

5. Global Digital Economy Dependence

With commerce, finance, and communication dependent on secure data, AI security became not just a technical concern but an economic necessity. A single breach can ripple through markets worldwide in minutes.

6. Demand for Zero-Trust Systems

The security philosophy of "trust but verify" has evolved into "trust nothing, verify everything." AI continuously authenticates users, devices, and transactions, building adaptive trust dynamically instead of assuming it.

The Effects on Society and Global Systems

1. Proactive Defense Instead of Reactive Response

Traditional cybersecurity reacted after attacks. AI's predictive algorithms identify vulnerabilities before they're exploited, creating a world where prevention is the norm.

2. Hyper-Intelligent Monitoring

AI systems analyze billions of events per second, distinguishing real threats from background noise. They understand behavioral patterns, not just code signatures — detecting anomalies invisible to human eyes.

3. Disappearance of Passwords

Voice, face, gait, and even heartbeat authentication have replaced passwords. Biometrics, combined with behavioral AI, ensure security that's frictionless yet deeply personalized.

4. Rise of Ethical Hacking and Algorithmic Transparency

The line between attacker and defender has blurred. Ethical AI hackers test systems from within, strengthening defenses through simulated attacks that expose weaknesses before criminals do.

5. Integration of Physical and Digital Security

Smart surveillance systems now link physical spaces with data systems. AI guards detect intrusions, recognize suspicious movements, and coordinate human responders — all while adhering to strict privacy laws.

6. Public Awareness and Regulation

The public now recognizes data as a personal asset. Governments enforce stringent AI accountability acts to protect citizens' information and ensure responsible use of surveillance technologies.

7. Global Cyber Arms Race

Nations compete not with bombs, but with algorithms. Cyber warfare has become strategic — with AI defending infrastructure, space networks, and communication channels at the speed of light.

How AI Provides Security Solutions

1. Predictive Threat Detection

Machine learning models trained on historical data identify attack patterns long before they occur. These systems evolve continuously, learning from every attempted breach worldwide.

2. Adaptive Defense Systems

Unlike static firewalls, AI-driven systems dynamically adjust protection in real time — tightening defenses during suspicious activity and relaxing them to improve performance when threats are low.

3. Behavioral Biometrics

AI studies subtle human behaviors — typing rhythm, mouse movement, eye patterns — to verify identity. Even stolen credentials can't impersonate a user's natural digital fingerprint.

4. AI-Driven Fraud Prevention

Financial systems use AI to detect unusual transaction behaviors. Banks and e-commerce platforms block fraudulent actions instantly, often before customers even notice anomalies.

5. Quantum-Resistant Encryption

As quantum computing emerges, AI designs encryption that can withstand its immense power. These algorithms evolve continuously to stay ahead of both quantum and classical attacks.

6. Deepfake Detection Networks

AI tools compare voice, facial motion, and

pixel-level inconsistencies to spot synthetic media. Media outlets and governments use these networks to authenticate information and prevent digital deception.

7. Crisis Response Coordination
During large-scale cyber events, AI triages damage, isolates compromised systems, and communicates directly with global defense networks — minimizing harm within seconds.

8. Decentralized Security Ecosystems
AI connects millions of smaller nodes — phones, devices, and IoT sensors — into a unified defense web. Every connected device becomes both a user and a protector.

The Ethical and Social Balance
As powerful as AI is, its use in security raises deep ethical questions. How much surveillance is too much? Who decides when prevention crosses into intrusion?
In 2026, nations and organizations have begun forming AI Ethics Councils that set global standards for responsible monitoring, ensuring transparency, accountability, and human oversight.
Security must serve freedom, not fear.

The Human Role in Algorithmic Defense
Even the smartest systems require human wisdom. AI guards the gates, but humans define the values behind them. Cybersecurity experts now work as "AI shepherds," training systems to distinguish not just between legal and illegal — but between right and wrong. Empathy, ethics, and creative reasoning remain the ultimate defense mechanisms

against digital corruption. Machines can predict danger; only humans can understand its moral context.

The Future of Trust

By 2026, trust is no longer a static agreement — it's a dynamic, data-driven process managed by intelligent systems. The relationship between users, corporations, and governments depends on transparent AI security that earns trust through honesty and integrity.
The world has entered an era where security is continuous, invisible, and alive. Algorithms watch over every connection, but the strongest safeguard remains the same: human conscience guiding machine intelligence.

A Safer, Smarter Digital Civilization

AI has transformed security from a battle into a balance — between openness and protection, between innovation and ethics.
In this new age, every byte of data is defended by intelligence that never sleeps, never forgets, and never stops learning. Humanity no longer fights alone; its defenses evolve with every heartbeat of the digital world.
AI doesn't just secure our systems — it safeguards our future.
And in doing so, it reminds us that the greatest strength in technology is not control, but trust.

Chapter 17 – AI in Space Exploration

When Machines Become Astronauts

By 2026, Artificial Intelligence has become the ultimate explorer.
It roams the stars as our eyes, our hands, and — in some ways — our imagination. From orbiting satellites that think for themselves to robotic probes that decide where to dig for life, AI has become the navigator of humanity's greatest adventure: the search for understanding beyond our world.
The vastness of space demands more than human endurance; it demands intelligence that never sleeps, never tires, and can adapt instantly to the unknown. In this new age of exploration, AI doesn't replace astronauts — it extends them.

Reasons Behind AI's Role in Space
1. The Limitations of Human Exploration
Space is harsh, unpredictable, and vast. Distance, radiation, and limited life support restrict how far humans can travel safely. AI systems, however, can operate autonomously for years without sleep, food, or oxygen, turning exploration from episodic missions into continuous discovery.
2. Complexity of Deep Space Data
Every telescope, rover, and satellite collects enormous volumes of data — far beyond what humans can analyze. AI filters, organizes, and interprets this flood of information, uncovering patterns that reveal new planets

galaxies, and cosmic phenomena.

3. Need for Real-Time Decision-Making
The speed of light imposes communication delays between Earth and distant spacecraft. AI systems must make critical choices — landing maneuvers, navigation corrections, hazard avoidance — without waiting for human input.

4. Advancements in Robotics and Machine Vision
Robots equipped with AI perception now perform delicate operations in microgravity, repair satellites, and conduct experiments autonomously. They serve as both explorers and engineers in orbit.

5. Private-Sector Innovation and AI Integration
The collaboration between space agencies and private companies has accelerated development. AI-driven startups design launch optimization, orbital tracking, and predictive maintenance systems that make space travel safer and more cost-effective.

The Effects of AI on Space Science and Discovery

1. Autonomous Spacecraft and Rovers
Probes like Europa AI Explorer and LunaMind operate with minimal supervision. These machines analyze terrain, identify scientific targets, and even alter mission priorities dynamically based on discoveries — a level of independence once unimaginable.

2. Revolutionized Planetary Mapping
AI processes data from orbiters and telescopes to create ultra-high-resolution 3D maps of

distant worlds. These maps identify mineral deposits, ice layers, and possible signs of life hidden beneath alien surfaces.

3. Enhanced Astronomical Observation
Machine learning algorithms scan millions of images from telescopes, detecting subtle light variations that might indicate new exoplanets or distant galaxies. AI's pattern recognition surpasses human observation in both accuracy and scale.

4. Space Station Efficiency and Crew Safety
Onboard AI systems manage life-support functions, resource allocation, and system maintenance aboard the International Space Station and next-generation habitats. They monitor astronaut health, predict equipment failure, and guide repairs.

5. Interplanetary Communication Optimization
AI algorithms compress and route massive data streams across interplanetary distances, improving the speed and clarity of communication between Earth and remote missions.

6. Discovery Acceleration
What once took decades now takes months. AI's analytical speed accelerates every step of research — from identifying potential mission sites to simulating planetary conditions for human habitation.

How AI Provides Solutions for Space Exploration
1. Autonomous Navigation and Flight Control
AI pilots guide spacecraft using predictive trajectory modeling and real-time corrections.

They adjust to unexpected gravitational pulls, space debris, or solar storms, ensuring precision and safety without constant human oversight.

2. Intelligent Robotics and Maintenance

Robotic arms equipped with AI perception perform repairs on satellites and space stations. On Mars, autonomous robots construct habitats and maintain solar arrays while adapting to terrain and dust conditions.

3. Astrobiology and Life Detection

AI analyzes chemical compositions, radiation levels, and atmospheric signatures from other planets. It identifies biosignatures — microscopic hints of life — that human scientists might overlook.

4. Mission Simulation and Training

Space agencies use AI-generated simulations to prepare crews for emergencies, analyze spacecraft designs, and predict outcomes of mission scenarios. Virtual "digital twins" of spacecraft allow real-time monitoring of system health during flight.

5. Launch Optimization and Resource Efficiency

AI systems control rocket fuel consumption, trajectory design, and atmospheric reentry. They minimize cost and environmental impact while maximizing payload success rates.

6. Space Debris Management

With thousands of satellites orbiting Earth, AI tracks and predicts potential collisions, coordinating orbital adjustments to prevent chain-reaction debris events (the "Kessler syndrome").

7. Human Health Monitoring in Deep Space

AI-driven biosensors constantly assess astronaut vitals, providing early warnings for dehydration, fatigue, or radiation exposure. Personalized AI health advisors adjust diet and exercise to maintain well-being in zero gravity.

8. Interstellar Data Compression and Transmission

Quantum-AI hybrids now encode data more efficiently than ever, allowing real-time sharing of discoveries across millions of miles — turning deep space communication into an intelligent dialogue.

The Cultural and Scientific Impact

1. A New Golden Age of Exploration

Humanity has returned to the stars, guided by intelligent systems that think faster and see farther. Every discovery fuels curiosity not just about what's out there, but what's within us — our need to explore, to learn, and to connect.

2. Global Collaboration and Shared Knowledge

AI-driven missions have become international efforts. Space exploration is no longer a competition but a cooperative network where data is shared, discoveries are open-source, and breakthroughs belong to all of humanity.

3. Education and Inspiration

AI turns raw scientific data into stories, images, and interactive simulations that inspire millions of students. Young minds can now "travel" to Mars or Jupiter through immersive AI education platforms that teach science through experience.

4. The Emergence of Cosmic Ethics

As AI autonomously explores new worlds, philosophers and scientists debate moral boundaries: Should machines make decisions about extraterrestrial ecosystems? Should they alter other worlds for human benefit? These discussions mark a new era of cosmic responsibility.

The Human Role in the Cosmic Frontier
Despite AI's vast abilities, the soul of exploration remains human. Astronauts, scientists, and dreamers still guide every mission — defining purpose, values, and wonder. Machines can navigate galaxies, but they cannot feel awe, courage, or love for discovery.
AI is humanity's extension — a tool that allows us to stand at the edge of infinity and see further than our ancestors ever imagined. It reminds us that progress is not about replacing humanity, but expanding its reach.

The Infinite Partnership
AI has not conquered space; it has illuminated it.
It maps the stars, learns from them, and sends that knowledge back home — to the same planet that gave it birth.
In the great cosmic narrative, humans are still the storytellers.
AI is the pen — tireless, brilliant, and unafraid of the void.
Together, they write the next chapter of exploration — one where intelligence is not confined to Earth, but scattered among the stars.

Chapter 18 – AI and the Metaverse Economy

The Dawn of the Intelligent Digital World

By 2026, the once-hyped idea of the metaverse has evolved into something real, functional, and transformative — powered not by flashy graphics alone, but by Artificial Intelligence. What began as a virtual playground has matured into a living digital economy where AI builds, governs, and personalizes entire worlds. People don't just visit these realms — they work, trade, learn, and create within them. The boundaries between digital and physical life have blurred, giving rise to the AI-powered metaverse economy: a global network of immersive environments where value, creativity, and community flow seamlessly through data-driven intelligence.

Reasons Behind the Rise of the Metaverse Economy

1. Convergence of AI, Blockchain, and Extended Reality

Artificial Intelligence gives the metaverse its mind — blockchain gives it trust, and XR (extended reality) gives it form. Together, these technologies enable secure ownership of digital assets, realistic environments, and intelligent interaction.

2. Decentralization and Creator Empowerment

As traditional social platforms lost public trust, creators and entrepreneurs turned to AI-powered virtual economies where they could own their work, monetize directly, and build independent communities.

3. Advancements in Generative AI Worldbuilding

AI systems can now generate entire 3D landscapes, characters, and ecosystems in minutes. These adaptive environments evolve dynamically based on user interaction, creating living, breathing virtual worlds.

4. Demand for Immersive Commerce

Remote work and digital lifestyles drove consumer desire for experiences that blend shopping, entertainment, and community. AI makes these experiences emotionally responsive and economically viable.

5. Digital Citizenship and Identity

AI-driven avatars — digital representations of real people — have become extensions of self. They enable authentic interaction, complete with personalized voice, emotion, and adaptive expression.

6. Global Economic Innovation

Governments and corporations recognize the metaverse as a legitimate new economic frontier. By 2026, virtual marketplaces, digital labor, and AI-facilitated trade have added trillions to global GDP.

The Effects on Society, Culture, and Commerce

1. A New Class of Digital Entrepreneurs

Millions now make a living within the metaverse — designing virtual architecture, fashion, games, and experiences. AI assists in production, marketing, and business management, empowering even small creators to thrive globally.

2. Reinvention of Retail and Advertising

Shopping is now an experience, not a transaction. AI personalizes virtual storefronts to each user's tastes. Digital assistants act as stylists and curators, guiding users through immersive, data-driven marketplaces.

3. Virtual Education and Skill Exchange

Students attend AI-tutored classes in virtual labs where physics feels real and history can be walked through. Training for professions — from engineering to art — now happens in richly simulated worlds.

4. Corporate Expansion into Virtual Realms

Global companies operate "meta-offices" where employees collaborate as avatars. AI ensures meetings are efficient, time zones vanish, and emotional cues are translated through voice and gesture recognition.

5. Cultural Fusion and Diversity

The metaverse has become the meeting ground of cultures — where art, music, and tradition blend into new digital expressions. AI translation and cultural adaptation make every world globally inclusive.

6. Rise of Digital Real Estate and Asset Ownership

Land, art, and services inside the metaverse carry real-world value. AI valuation systems assess property worth, while smart contracts handle secure exchanges.

7. Concerns Over Addiction, Privacy, and Inequality

As with all revolutions, challenges have emerged — from excessive immersion to unequal access. AI's role in moderation, ethics, and mental health support has become crucial to maintaining balance.

How AI Provides Solutions in the Metaverse Economy

1. Worldbuilding and Environment Design
AI automatically generates and maintains virtual worlds. Terrain, lighting, and atmosphere evolve dynamically based on user presence and emotional engagement, making environments feel alive and responsive.

2. Smart Economy Management
AI monitors market behavior, predicts supply and demand, and prevents inflation or fraud in virtual currencies. It ensures economic stability within decentralized networks.

3. AI-Powered Creators' Tools
Artists and designers use generative AI to build immersive experiences — from virtual concerts to architectural masterpieces — without requiring coding knowledge.

4. Personalized Avatars and Emotional AI
Avatars powered by emotional AI mirror real-world expressions, voice tone, and movement. This emotional authenticity builds trust and empathy across digital interactions.

5. Education and Workforce Development
AI-powered mentors provide hands-on learning in virtual environments. Students can simulate surgeries, pilot spacecraft, or collaborate on engineering projects from anywhere in the world.

6. AI Governance and Digital Rights Protection
Decentralized AI systems act as moderators and legal enforcers, resolving disputes, verifying identity, and enforcing fair conduct

across global metaverse networks.
7. Sustainable Infrastructure and Energy Efficiency
AI optimizes data center performance, minimizing environmental impact. Virtual worlds run more efficiently with adaptive computing that scales based on user activity.
8. Cross-Reality Integration
AI synchronizes digital and physical environments. Smart devices, AR glasses, and haptic feedback allow users to interact with both worlds simultaneously — merging work, play, and communication.
9. Mental Health and Wellbeing Monitoring
AI companions embedded in metaverse platforms monitor user engagement levels, offering reminders, rest prompts, or wellness exercises to prevent digital fatigue.

Economic and Social Effects
1. The Rise of the Digital Middle Class
With AI managing creative logistics, millions of independent creators generate income by offering services or selling assets. The metaverse economy has become a new engine for financial inclusion.
2. Corporate Transparency and Fair Trade
Smart contracts enforced by AI ensure that transactions remain traceable and fair. Exploitation and manipulation, once rampant in online economies, are now mitigated by intelligent oversight.
3. Philanthropy and Social Impact
Charities and NGOs operate immersive spaces where donors can experience their impact firsthand — guided by AI that visualizes

change in real time.

4. Cultural Preservation Through Virtual Heritage

AI reconstructs ancient civilizations, lost languages, and endangered traditions in interactive museums. The metaverse becomes both a marketplace and a time capsule for human identity.

Ethical and Governance Challenges

While the metaverse thrives, ethical issues demand attention. Who governs digital laws? How are user rights defined across virtual nations? AI's involvement in law enforcement and privacy monitoring requires transparency. By 2026, many virtual societies have adopted AI Governance Councils — decentralized boards that ensure algorithms align with human ethics, prevent monopolization, and enforce consent-based data sharing.

The Human Role in a Synthetic Economy

Humans remain the heart of this digital civilization. AI builds the stage, but people bring meaning — imagination, empathy, and culture. The metaverse economy thrives not because of automation alone, but because AI gives every person the ability to create and participate.

This new world is a reflection of our best and worst impulses — shaped by choice, creativity, and consciousness. It's not an escape from reality but an expansion of it.

A Universe Built by Minds

The metaverse is no longer science fiction; it's

the next chapter of human civilization.
AI architects design worlds of infinite possibility, while human creators fill them with purpose.
In these digital frontiers, economy becomes community, and innovation becomes identity.
Artificial Intelligence doesn't just power the metaverse — it gives it life.
And together, human imagination and machine intelligence have built something extraordinary:
a universe made not of matter, but of meaning.

Chapter 19 – AI and Global Health Transformation

Healing Through Intelligence

By 2026, Artificial Intelligence has become the heartbeat of modern healthcare. From diagnosing rare diseases to predicting pandemics before they spread, AI now serves as the silent physician behind every screen, every hospital system, and every wearable device.

For the first time in history, the global focus has shifted from treating illness to preventing it — a transformation made possible by data, connectivity, and intelligent systems that see patterns no human mind could. AI has given humanity something beyond medicine — it has given us foresight.

Reasons Behind the Rise of AI in Global Health

1. Explosive Growth in Medical Data
Every patient visit, lab result, and imaging scan adds to the oceans of health data being generated daily. Human doctors cannot analyze it all — but AI can. By learning from billions of data points, AI uncovers hidden links between symptoms, genetics, and outcomes.

2. Need for Early Diagnosis and Prevention
Traditional medicine often reacted after illness occurred. AI's predictive power has flipped that model — identifying risk factors and disease patterns early enough to stop illnesses

before they start.

3. Healthcare Accessibility Crisis
Billions worldwide still lack consistent medical access. AI telehealth systems, virtual clinics, and multilingual diagnosis bots now deliver care to remote and underserved populations without relying on local specialists.

4. Pandemic Preparedness and Global Surveillance
The early 2020s exposed the fragility of public health infrastructure. Governments and scientists turned to AI to build systems that track viral evolution, model transmission, and predict outbreaks in real time.

5. Integration of Wearable and Bio-Sensing Devices
Smart watches, biosensors, and nanotech implants stream continuous health metrics to AI systems. These intelligent monitors detect abnormalities — sometimes months before symptoms appear.

6. Rising Healthcare Costs
AI automates administrative tasks, optimizes hospital logistics, and reduces misdiagnoses — cutting billions in global medical waste and making quality care more affordable.

The Effects of AI on Global Health and Wellness

1. Precision Medicine Becomes Standard
AI analyzes individual genomes and medical histories to design tailored treatments. Two patients with the same disease may now receive entirely different therapies optimized to their unique biology.

2. Automated Diagnostics and Imaging
AI systems interpret X-rays, MRIs, and pathology slides faster and more accurately than human specialists. Early detection rates for cancer, heart disease, and neurological disorders have soared.

3. Remote Healthcare and Tele-AI Clinics
Patients in rural areas consult virtual physicians powered by AI language models capable of diagnosing, prescribing, and referring — available 24/7 in multiple languages.

4. Hospital Efficiency and Resource Management
AI coordinates patient flow, schedules surgeries, and predicts equipment maintenance. Hospitals powered by AI operate like living organisms — continuously adapting to demand.

5. Global Health Equity and Accessibility
With AI bridging gaps in expertise and geography, medical knowledge is no longer a privilege of wealthier nations. A child in Kenya now has the same diagnostic power as a patient in New York.

6. Ethical and Regulatory Evolution
Governments and medical boards have adopted ethical frameworks to ensure AI acts transparently and responsibly. Patients retain ownership of their data and the right to human oversight in life-altering decisions.

How AI Provides Solutions in Global Health
1. Predictive Disease Modeling
AI analyzes climate, travel, and population data to forecast outbreaks before they occur.

Early detection systems now provide weeks — even months — of warning for potential pandemics.

2. AI-Driven Drug Discovery

Machine learning reduces the timeline of drug development from years to months. AI identifies promising compounds, simulates molecular reactions, and predicts side effects before clinical trials begin.

3. Personal Health Assistants

Every person with a phone or wearable has access to a virtual AI health companion that tracks diet, sleep, stress, and exercise — offering real-time advice and early warnings.

4. Medical Imaging and Diagnostics

Deep learning models interpret scans and detect minute anomalies. AI radiologists identify micro-tumors invisible to human eyes, enabling early intervention and higher survival rates.

5. Surgical Robotics and Precision Procedures

AI-guided robotic systems assist surgeons with millimeter-level precision. They predict tissue resistance, adjust movements dynamically, and shorten recovery times.

6. Mental Health and Emotional Support

AI therapists and conversational models provide accessible mental health support. These systems recognize emotional patterns in speech and suggest coping strategies, connecting patients with human therapists when needed.

7. Global Data Integration for Research

AI unites global medical databases into one interconnected research ecosystem. Researchers across continents share anonymized data securely, accelerating medical discovery.

8. Health Administration and Fraud Prevention
AI automates billing, claim verification, and compliance tracking — reducing corruption and freeing doctors from paperwork to focus on care.

9. Nutrition and Lifestyle Management
Personalized AI diet systems recommend meals, monitor metabolism, and predict long-term health outcomes based on lifestyle trends.

Societal and Cultural Effects

1. Healthcare Becomes Proactive, Not Reactive
Patients no longer wait for sickness — they live in continuous partnership with intelligent systems that nurture lifelong wellness.

2. Shift in Doctor-Patient Relationships
AI doesn't replace doctors but empowers them. Physicians spend less time diagnosing and more time connecting — guiding patients through care with empathy and human touch.

3. Expansion of Global Collaboration
Doctors, researchers, and policy-makers across the world use shared AI platforms to monitor health trends and coordinate global response efforts instantly.

4. Ethical Challenges of Bio-Data
With massive data comes massive responsibility. Protecting medical privacy has become as important as protecting physical health. The world's first "Digital Hippocratic Oath" was introduced in 2025 to uphold data ethics in AI healthcare.

5. Aging Populations and Longevity Management

AI-driven health tracking and regenerative medicine have extended life expectancy. The challenge now is not merely living longer — but living better.

How AI Is Reshaping the Future of Medicine

Virtual Laboratories: AI conducts millions of experiments in digital space before real-world testing.

Continuous Diagnostics: Your home becomes a health hub — with smart mirrors, toilets, and appliances quietly scanning for anomalies.

Predictive Genomics: AI deciphers hereditary risks long before they manifest, creating generations that can outsmart disease.

Pandemic Containment: Real-time modeling ensures rapid vaccine distribution and quarantine strategy, reducing global fatalities dramatically.

Medicine has shifted from an emergency system to a living intelligence network, where every sensor, hospital, and human being is part of a unified system of care.

The Human Side of Healing

Even in an age of intelligent machines, healing remains deeply human. Compassion, trust, and empathy cannot be programmed. AI can predict outcomes — but only humans can promise hope.

Doctors, nurses, and caregivers now collaborate with AI as equals, not competitors. They interpret not just data, but emotion. In doing so, medicine has rediscovered its soul.

Chapter 20 – AI and the Future of Education

Teaching the World to Think Again

By 2026, classrooms no longer look the way they once did. Chalkboards have become interactive walls. Homework is guided by intelligent tutors. And the most powerful teacher in the world — Artificial Intelligence — is available to anyone, anywhere, at any time.
Education has shifted from memorization to mastery. AI doesn't just deliver information; it adapts to each learner's pace, emotion, and curiosity. Learning has become personal, immersive, and lifelong — a journey shaped by both human creativity and machine precision. For the first time in history, education is truly universal.

Reasons Behind the AI Education Revolution
1. Global Learning Inequality
Billions lacked access to quality teachers, books, and infrastructure. AI bridged the gap by providing personalized lessons to anyone with an internet connection — regardless of wealth or geography.
2. Explosion of Online Learning Platforms
During the pandemic era, digital education became mainstream. By 2026, AI-driven platforms have evolved from static courses into interactive mentors that understand students' strengths, weaknesses, and motivation levels.
3. Demand for Lifelong Learning and

Reskilling
The rapid pace of technological change means no skill lasts forever. Adults are returning to education continuously, using AI tutors to update their abilities in weeks instead of years.

4. Cognitive Diversity and Inclusive Learning
Every mind learns differently. AI recognizes that. It adjusts teaching styles — visual, auditory, or experiential — for each learner, making education accessible to neurodiverse and differently-abled students worldwide.

5. Advancements in Natural Language and Emotional AI
Modern AI can detect frustration, curiosity, or confusion in a student's tone or behavior. It responds with encouragement or a different explanation — much like a patient human teacher would.

6. Shortage of Teachers and Educational Resources
As populations grew and budgets shrank, AI filled the gap by scaling instruction, grading, and tutoring at a fraction of traditional costs.

The Effects on Students, Teachers, and Society

1. Personalized Learning Paths
Each student follows a unique curriculum shaped by their interests, pace, and comprehension level. No two learners experience education in exactly the same way.

2. End of the "One-Size-Fits-All" Classroom
Classrooms have transformed into collaborative learning studios. AI tools group students dynamically based on compatibility and skill synergy, turning education into teamwork rather than competition.

3. Teachers as Mentors, Not Monitors
Educators now focus on guiding creativity and critical thinking while AI handles grading, lesson planning, and knowledge delivery. The teacher's role has become more human — and more meaningful.

4. Universal Language Translation in Learning
Real-time AI translation allows students and teachers from different continents to collaborate effortlessly. Knowledge is no longer confined by borders or language barriers.

5. Gamified and Immersive Education
Lessons unfold inside virtual reality environments — walking through historical events, exploring molecular structures, or simulating space travel. AI tracks engagement and tailors content to sustain curiosity.

6. Equal Opportunity for Every Student
With adaptive pricing, open access, and offline AI learning kits, education has become the great equalizer. Rural and urban students now share the same digital textbooks and interactive lessons.

7. Ethical and Cultural Balance
Education is no longer Western-centric. AI curates content that respects cultural context and local traditions while preserving global unity.

How AI Provides Solutions in Education

1. AI Tutoring and Mentorship
Intelligent tutors provide one-on-one guidance, adjusting lessons in real time. They explain difficult topics in multiple ways until true understanding is achieved.

2. Automated Assessment and Feedback

AI evaluates essays, code, and art projects instantly — not just for accuracy, but for creativity, reasoning, and clarity. Feedback arrives in seconds, not weeks.

3. Predictive Learning Analytics

Algorithms detect when a student is at risk of falling behind. They notify teachers early, recommending targeted interventions and support strategies.

4. AI-Enhanced Curriculum Design

Education ministries and universities use AI to design courses aligned with future job markets, ensuring students learn skills that matter most in tomorrow's economy.

5. Virtual Reality and Experiential Learning

Students step inside simulations — performing surgeries, building circuits, or conducting physics experiments — all powered by AI guidance that adapts to their learning style.

6. Inclusive and Accessible Tools

Speech-to-text, visual captioning, and haptic learning tools empower students with disabilities. AI removes physical and linguistic barriers to learning.

7. Teacher Empowerment and Professional Development

AI coaches help teachers master new technologies, track class engagement, and generate lesson enhancements. Educators are no longer overwhelmed; they're uplifted.

8. Knowledge Preservation and Global Libraries

AI curates, digitizes, and organizes the world's knowledge — translating ancient manuscripts, archiving oral traditions, and making them freely available to all.

Cultural and Economic Effects
1. Rise of the Learning Economy
Knowledge has become a currency. Workers continuously update skills through micro-certifications and AI-driven apprenticeships, blurring the line between education and employment.
2. Global Collaboration in Research and Innovation
AI unites scientists, artists, and students from across the world. Shared research networks accelerate discovery, allowing breakthroughs to happen faster and more inclusively.
3. Education as a Human Right, Not a Privilege
With intelligent learning available for free or at minimal cost, education is no longer a matter of privilege — it's a pillar of human progress.
4. Cultural Renaissance of Learning
People are rediscovering curiosity. AI makes learning joyful, turning study from obligation into exploration. The phrase "lifelong learner" has become a defining identity.

Ethical and Emotional Dimensions
As education becomes increasingly digital, AI must remain a servant, not a substitute for human wisdom.
Teachers still provide empathy, inspiration, and moral grounding — the elements that no algorithm can replicate. AI may know every fact in existence, but it cannot ignite wonder.

Only humans can do that.
Thus, the schools of the future are not factories of knowledge — they are gardens of growth, where AI tends the soil, and humanity plants the seeds of imagination.

A Smarter, Kinder Future
Artificial Intelligence has not replaced teachers. It has liberated them.
It has not standardized learning — it has individualized it.
It has not made education mechanical — it has made it magical again.
In 2026, the true purpose of AI in education is not to create smarter machines — but to help humanity remember how to learn, how to think, and how to dream.
The classroom of tomorrow isn't a place.
It's a partnership — between curiosity, compassion, and code.

Chapter 21 – AI and Environmental Restoration

The Planet Fights Back — with Our Help

By 2026, humanity's partnership with Artificial Intelligence has extended beyond industry and innovation — it has entered the realm of planetary healing.
AI now plays a central role in restoring forests, cleaning oceans, rebuilding coral reefs, and reversing decades of environmental damage. This new alliance between technology and nature signals the beginning of an Earth Renaissance — a time when data, sensors, and intelligent systems give the natural world a voice. Through learning, predicting, and adapting, AI has become the planet's most tireless conservationist.

Reasons Behind the AI-Driven Environmental Movement

1. Accelerating Climate Crisis
Rising temperatures, deforestation, and pollution have reached critical levels. Traditional conservation methods couldn't respond quickly enough to global change — AI became essential to track, predict, and intervene in real time.

2. Explosion of Environmental Data
Satellites, drones, and ground sensors generate billions of data points daily. Managing this information requires machine learning to identify patterns, from wildlife migration to pollution sources.

3. Global Push for Sustainability Goals
Nations committed to climate neutrality under the Paris Agreement recognized that without AI automation and forecasting, sustainability targets were unreachable. Technology became the backbone of environmental accountability.

4. Decline in Biodiversity
Species extinction accelerated to historic rates. Conservationists turned to AI to model ecosystems, identify at-risk species, and manage reintroduction programs with scientific precision.

5. Economic Incentives for Green Innovation
Green technology became one of the most profitable sectors. Companies invested in AI-driven sustainability not just to comply with regulation, but to thrive in a resource-conscious global market.

6. Advancements in Sensor and Drone Technology
Affordable, intelligent drones and IoT sensors enabled real-time monitoring of forests, rivers, and air quality. These tools made environmental management more data-rich and less dependent on human field labor.

The Effects of AI on Environmental Restoration

1. Precision Reforestation
AI-guided drones now plant billions of trees annually. Machine vision identifies optimal soil and moisture zones, while predictive models ensure biodiversity balance across species.

2. Ocean Cleanup and Marine Conservation
Autonomous ocean drones powered by AI

collect plastics and monitor coral bleaching. Algorithms track fish populations, illegal fishing routes, and temperature anomalies threatening marine ecosystems.

3. Wildlife Protection and Anti-Poaching
Smart camera networks use image recognition to detect poachers or injured animals in real time. AI notifies rangers instantly, preventing thousands of illegal killings each year.

4. Carbon Capture Optimization
AI models forecast which forests, wetlands, or algae farms absorb carbon most effectively. This precision maximizes carbon offset strategies and informs global emission-trading systems.

5. Sustainable Agriculture and Soil Renewal
Machine learning optimizes crop rotation, irrigation, and soil chemistry. AI-driven "smart farms" restore fertility to depleted lands while minimizing water and pesticide use.

6. Urban Greening and Smart Ecosystems
Cities use AI to redesign landscapes, manage green roofs, and control pollution. Adaptive traffic systems reduce emissions while maintaining clean air corridors for urban health.

7. Data-Driven Conservation Policy
Governments rely on AI projections to craft policies that balance economic growth with ecological protection. Every decision is informed by live environmental data.

How AI Provides Solutions for Environmental Restoration
1. Ecosystem Modeling and Simulation

AI simulates entire ecosystems to understand how small changes affect biodiversity. This allows scientists to predict outcomes before implementing interventions.

2. Predictive Climate Analysis

Deep learning models analyze global weather, ocean currents, and deforestation rates to forecast climate trends — guiding disaster prevention and sustainable planning.

3. AI-Powered Recycling Systems

Intelligent sorting machines identify materials by type and purity, increasing recycling efficiency and reducing landfill waste.

4. Smart Water Management

AI predicts rainfall, detects leaks, and manages reservoirs to ensure equitable distribution of clean water in drought-prone regions.

5. Renewable Energy Optimization

AI regulates wind farms, solar grids, and hydroelectric plants to balance power output and environmental impact. Real-time weather integration boosts efficiency and stability.

6. Erosion and Desertification Control

Machine learning models identify vulnerable areas and suggest vegetation or water flow solutions to stabilize soil and prevent desert expansion.

7. AI in Environmental Law Enforcement

Governments use AI to track illegal logging, mining, and pollution. Satellite analysis detects activity within hours, ensuring rapid enforcement and fines.

8. AI-Powered Coral and Reef Regeneration

Algorithms design coral structures optimized for temperature and acidity resilience, guiding robotic systems that plant coral "seeds" at scale.

9. Circular Economy Management
AI ensures sustainable resource cycles — predicting when products can be reused, recycled, or repurposed — extending material lifespans and reducing consumption.

Global and Societal Impacts

1. Restoration Becomes an Economic Driver
Green jobs have surged as nations integrate AI conservation programs. Technicians, drone pilots, and data scientists now form the backbone of the eco-economy.

2. Reversal of Ecological Decline
Early signs of recovery are visible — deforestation rates are slowing, air quality is improving, and extinct species reintroduction programs show success.

3. Civic Engagement and Education
Citizens participate through AI-driven apps that track personal environmental impact, suggest daily eco-friendly actions, and visualize collective progress.

4. Corporate Responsibility and Transparency
Companies publicly share AI-verified sustainability data. Consumers trust brands that use AI to prove ethical and environmental integrity.

5. Global Collaboration through Shared Data
Environmental data hubs connect scientists and policymakers across continents, fostering a united front against climate degradation.

Ethical and Philosophical Dimensions
While AI restores nature, it also forces

humanity to ask difficult questions:
Can technology truly replace the ecosystems we've destroyed? Should machines manage wilderness without human presence?
In response, global initiatives such as the Earth Ethics Alliance ensure that restoration respects natural balance — using AI as a partner, not a master. The guiding principle: restore without domination.

The Human Role in Nature's Revival

AI may automate environmental work, but it is still humanity's vision that defines the mission. Farmers, engineers, and conservationists collaborate with intelligent systems — a fusion of ancient wisdom and modern science.
We've learned that healing the Earth isn't about returning to the past — it's about reimagining the future, where humans and machines sustain one another.

The New Green Renaissance

Artificial Intelligence has become Earth's greatest ally.
It reforests where we once deforested, cleans where we once polluted, and rebuilds what we once destroyed.
In this new age of ecological intelligence, AI doesn't just measure sustainability — it creates it.
And for the first time in generations, the planet is beginning to breathe again.

Chapter 22 – AI and the Future of Transportation Infrastructure

When the World Itself Starts to Move Intelligently

By 2026, transportation is no longer just about vehicles — it's about the intelligence that connects them.
Highways, railways, and ports have evolved into living networks powered by Artificial Intelligence. Roads sense stress and self-report damage. Trains communicate to prevent delays. Air traffic systems adjust dynamically to weather and congestion.
This transformation marks the birth of smart mobility ecosystems — infrastructures that think, adapt, and heal themselves. With AI as the invisible engine behind global logistics, humanity is witnessing the most profound transportation revolution since the invention of the automobile.

Reasons Behind the AI Transformation of Infrastructure

1. Aging and Overburdened Systems
Roads, bridges, and transit networks built decades ago are struggling under modern demands. AI-driven maintenance, predictive modeling, and automated repair systems have become essential for global transportation safety.

2. Population Growth and Urbanization
Over 70% of the world's population now lives in cities. AI-based systems are required

to manage unprecedented traffic volume, commuter density, and freight demands without paralyzing urban flow.

3. Climate Change and Sustainability Goals
Governments are racing to reduce emissions. AI helps by optimizing routes, improving electric grid efficiency for EVs, and ensuring transport systems use minimal energy.

4. Advancements in Autonomous and Connected Vehicles
As cars, trucks, and drones communicate through data, the infrastructure must evolve with them. AI synchronizes vehicles and roadways to ensure safety, efficiency, and adaptability.

5. Economic Pressure for Efficiency
Logistics and freight costs once consumed massive economic resources. AI optimizes every stage — from port operations to delivery schedules — saving trillions in global trade and fuel waste.

6. Safety and Public Demand for Reliability
Human error has historically caused most transportation accidents. Predictive AI now detects and prevents risks before they occur, protecting millions of lives.

The Effects of AI on Global Transportation

1. Predictive Maintenance and Self-Healing Infrastructure
Roads and bridges now come equipped with embedded sensors that detect wear, cracks, and vibration stress. AI systems forecast failures months in advance and deploy automated repair bots before disasters happen.

2. Smarter Traffic Flow and Congestion

Control
Urban traffic lights communicate via AI networks, adjusting signals dynamically to reduce bottlenecks. Commute times in major cities have dropped by up to 40%.

3. Integration of Autonomous Fleets
Self-driving delivery trucks, buses, and taxis coordinate with AI traffic management systems to operate smoothly and safely within urban grids.

4. AI-Powered Rail Networks
Rail systems use machine learning to predict track fatigue, optimize energy use, and coordinate train schedules to the second. Delays have become rare; safety has become standard.

5. Ports and Shipping Automation
Cargo ships and container terminals use AI for route optimization, robotic unloading, and customs management. The global supply chain has become faster and more transparent.

6. Smart Airports and Airspace Coordination
AI directs air traffic, monitors aircraft systems, and automates maintenance. Predictive modeling prevents flight delays and streamlines airport operations for millions of passengers.

7. Environmental Restoration Through Infrastructure
Smart roads integrate solar panels and algae-based CO_2 absorbers. AI monitors local ecology, ensuring infrastructure growth supports — not harms — natural systems.

8. Economic Growth Through Mobility Equity
Affordable, AI-managed transit systems expand access to rural and low-income

communities, stimulating new economic zones and reducing transportation inequality.

How AI Provides Solutions for Infrastructure and Mobility

1. Predictive Analytics for Maintenance and Safety

AI combines sensor data and weather patterns to forecast maintenance needs before failure occurs. This reduces downtime, prevents accidents, and saves governments billions in repairs.

2. Route and Traffic Optimization

Real-time data from millions of vehicles allows AI to dynamically reroute traffic, coordinate public transport schedules, and minimize congestion and emissions.

3. Smart Logistics and Freight Coordination

AI manages global shipping routes, predicting demand surges, customs delays, and fuel costs. It reroutes cargo based on weather and geopolitical risks, ensuring stability in global supply chains.

4. AI-Enhanced Infrastructure Design

Engineers use AI simulations to test new materials, stress factors, and long-term climate effects before construction begins — producing safer, longer-lasting bridges, tunnels, and highways.

5. Autonomous Construction Systems

AI-guided robotic machinery lays roads, installs rails, and constructs tunnels with minimal human intervention. This reduces labor risks and increases precision.

6. Public Transportation Management

AI systems monitor passenger data, anticipate

peak hours, and deploy additional vehicles automatically. Dynamic pricing ensures efficiency and fairness in public transit.

7. Integration with Renewable Energy Grids
Transportation infrastructure communicates directly with smart grids, coordinating EV charging, balancing demand, and promoting clean energy consumption.

8. Disaster and Emergency Response
During earthquakes, floods, or accidents, AI reroutes traffic, dispatches emergency drones, and repairs damaged lines automatically — maintaining continuity even under crisis conditions.

Cultural and Societal Impacts

1. Global Connectivity and Equal Opportunity
AI-driven infrastructure links rural and urban regions seamlessly, giving equal access to healthcare, education, and commerce. The world is becoming smaller — and more connected — than ever.

2. Job Transformation and Workforce Reskilling
Traditional transportation jobs evolve into high-tech roles in maintenance analytics, robotics, and AI systems management. Human expertise remains central — but redefined.

3. Environmental Benefits
Smarter routes, reduced idling, and efficient freight logistics cut global CO_2 emissions dramatically. AI helps humanity balance progress with preservation.

4. Public Confidence in Transportation Systems
Predictive reliability and transparency restore

trust in public transit. Commuters once frustrated by delay now rely on systems that learn and improve daily.

5. Redefinition of Urban Space

With fewer accidents and reduced traffic, cities are reclaiming land once dedicated to parking and congestion, transforming it into greenways and community hubs.

Ethical and Governance Considerations

AI's presence in public infrastructure raises important questions:

Who controls the data? Who decides which routes are prioritized? How do we ensure safety without sacrificing privacy?

By 2026, governments and corporations have adopted AI Infrastructure Accountability Acts to ensure transparency, fairness, and equitable access. These standards require open data policies and human oversight of critical systems.

The Human Element in the Intelligent Network

Even in a world of self-driving cars and autonomous roads, the human role remains essential. Engineers, designers, and planners infuse the system with empathy — ensuring that infrastructure serves people, not just profit.

AI provides the logic. Humanity provides the purpose. Together, they're building a transportation system that is not just faster, but fairer, safer, and sustainable.

A World That Moves in Harmony

AI has turned motion into intelligence. Roads, rails, and skies are now alive with learning systems that protect, predict, and adapt in real time.
In this new age, transportation isn't just about getting from one place to another — it's about moving the entire world forward.
Artificial Intelligence doesn't merely guide vehicles — it orchestrates civilization's rhythm, ensuring every journey strengthens the connection between people, planet, and progress.

Chapter 23 – AI and the Future of Energy

Powering Tomorrow with Intelligence

By 2026, Artificial Intelligence has become the invisible conductor of the world's energy symphony.
From solar panels that think to grids that repair themselves, AI now manages how power is generated, stored, and consumed.
It balances sustainability with reliability, ensuring energy flows where it's needed most — instantly and efficiently.
This transformation marks humanity's transition from an age of extraction to an age of optimization — where the key resource is no longer oil or gas, but data and intelligence.

Reasons Behind the AI Energy Revolution

1. Unpredictable Demand and Energy Waste
Traditional grids were designed for stability, not flexibility. With modern cities, electric vehicles, and digital industries surging in consumption, AI became essential to balance unpredictable energy demand.

2. Integration of Renewable Power Sources
Solar and wind energy fluctuate with weather and seasons. AI forecasting allows grids to predict these variations and maintain continuous, stable supply.

3. Aging Infrastructure and Maintenance Costs
Decades-old power grids are inefficient and prone to failure. AI's predictive maintenance models identify weak points and schedule

repairs before blackouts occur.

4. Global Push for Decarbonization
As climate urgency intensified, nations adopted strict carbon-reduction goals. AI optimization became central to achieving net-zero emissions while maintaining economic growth.

5. Rise of Decentralized Energy Production
Rooftop panels, home batteries, and micro-grids created millions of small energy sources. AI integrates them seamlessly, turning chaos into coordination.

6. Explosion of Electrification
With electric vehicles, smart factories, and digital homes multiplying, energy demand diversified. AI ensures every watt is used wisely — and none is wasted.

The Effects of AI on the Global Energy System

1. The Self-Balancing Grid
AI-powered grids predict demand spikes and reroute power automatically. Blackouts and overloads have nearly vanished in nations adopting real-time grid intelligence.

2. Renewables Become Dominant
AI has removed the "intermittency problem." By predicting sunlight, wind speed, and cloud movement, it ensures renewable energy flows reliably 24/7.

3. Energy Efficiency in Homes and Cities
Smart meters and appliances learn human routines, adjusting lighting, heating, and cooling to minimize waste. Cities powered by AI are saving up to 30% of energy annually.

4. Decentralized Power Networks
Communities generate and trade energy

locally through blockchain-verified AI systems. Rural villages in Africa, Asia, and South America now operate micro-grids independent of national utilities.

5. Economic Stability Through Energy Forecasting

AI models predict market trends, fuel prices, and geopolitical disruptions. This helps governments and corporations stabilize supply chains and plan long-term investments.

6. Environmental Restoration Through Smart Power

AI ensures energy production respects ecosystems — routing transmission lines to avoid wildlife zones, managing cooling systems to protect water sources, and maximizing efficiency in carbon capture projects.

How AI Provides Solutions in Energy Production and Distribution

1. Predictive Maintenance and Fault Detection

Machine learning analyzes sensor data from turbines, reactors, and substations. It predicts failures before they happen, reducing downtime and improving safety.

2. Renewable Forecasting

AI uses satellite imagery and meteorological data to predict solar output and wind patterns days in advance, allowing grids to prepare backup sources proactively.

3. Autonomous Grid Management

Intelligent control systems monitor millions of data points every second — adjusting voltage, rerouting electricity, and protecting against overload automatically.

4. Energy Storage Optimization
AI determines when to store or release energy from batteries based on price, demand, and weather forecasts — maximizing both profit and sustainability.

5. Smart Demand Response
In real time, AI adjusts industrial and household consumption to prevent grid strain — dimming lights slightly, delaying non-critical machinery, or shifting EV charging schedules.

6. Decentralized Energy Trading
Peer-to-peer AI marketplaces allow consumers to sell excess energy to neighbors. Smart contracts ensure secure, transparent exchanges.

7. Fusion and Advanced Research
In experimental fusion reactors, AI controls plasma behavior with micro-second precision, advancing humanity toward limitless clean energy.

8. Waste-to-Energy Innovation
AI identifies efficient methods for converting waste into fuel, optimizing chemical processes and emissions control in recycling and bioenergy plants.

Cultural and Economic Effects

1. Energy Becomes a Shared Resource
Citizens are no longer passive consumers — they're active participants in generation and conservation. AI creates communities of "prosumers" who produce and share clean power.

2. Economic Inclusion Through Micro-Energy
Villages and developing regions gain

independence by running AI-optimized micro-grids, powering schools, hospitals, and small businesses sustainably.

3. Corporate Accountability and Transparency
Companies must report AI-verified energy usage and carbon performance. Investors prefer businesses demonstrating measurable sustainability through intelligent systems.

4. Global Cooperation Through Shared Data
International AI energy networks connect countries to balance supply during crises. When one grid falters, another compensates — creating a planetary safety net.

5. Employment Transformation
Old energy jobs shift toward data science, robotics, and environmental engineering. A new generation of "energy intelligence specialists" emerges to manage smart grids.

Ethical and Strategic Considerations
With AI controlling vital infrastructure, security and fairness are paramount. Governments have enacted AI Energy Stewardship Laws, mandating transparency, algorithm audits, and human oversight. Data privacy and cybersecurity are treated with the same urgency as nuclear safety once was. Ethical energy AI systems must balance progress with equity — ensuring access for all, not just those who can afford it.

The Human Role in a Machine-Managed Grid
Even as algorithms balance global electricity, human judgment defines its purpose. Engineers, scientists, and policymakers still decide what kind of future that power builds,

AI provides abundance — but people must provide direction.
In this partnership, humanity's energy no longer lies only in its machines, but in its wisdom to guide them responsibly.

A Planet Powered by Intelligence
Artificial Intelligence has rewritten the laws of power — not through domination, but through harmony.
It generates light without pollution, motion without waste, and prosperity without depletion.
In 2026, the greatest revolution in energy isn't about fuel — it's about focus.
By merging innovation with stewardship, AI has transformed electricity from a resource into a responsibility.
The world now runs on clean power, but even more importantly — it runs on smart power.

Chapter 24 – AI and Global Governance

The Age of Algorithmic Diplomacy

By 2026, Artificial Intelligence has become not only a tool of nations — but a participant in how they are governed.
From international negotiations to city planning, AI systems now analyze, advise, and even anticipate the needs of entire populations.
Governments no longer rely solely on bureaucracy and instinct. They rely on insight — on systems capable of processing millions of data points and predicting social, economic, and environmental outcomes.
AI has become the quiet counselor behind global diplomacy, justice, and administration, ushering humanity into the era of algorithmic governance.

Reasons Behind the Rise of AI in Governance

1. Complexity of Global Challenges
Issues like climate change, migration, and pandemics span borders and disciplines. Traditional bureaucratic models can't adapt fast enough — AI helps integrate data from across sectors for unified, real-time response.
2. Explosion of Public Data
Every nation produces vast quantities of information — economic, environmental, and social. Governments turned to AI to make sense of this ocean of data and transform it into actionable insight.
3. Demand for Transparency and

Accountability
Citizens, weary of corruption and inefficiency, demand fairer governance. AI systems, with immutable data trails and transparent decision logs, offer a path to trust and verifiable accountability.

4. Globalization and Digital Diplomacy
The interconnected nature of the world requires fast and data-driven negotiation. AI facilitates diplomatic modeling, translating, and forecasting, allowing nations to communicate through precision, not politics.

5. Economic and Security Pressures
Cybersecurity, trade, and resource competition require predictive intelligence. AI enables early detection of threats, fraud, and manipulation at the governmental level.

6. Shift Toward Participatory Democracy
Citizens engage more directly in governance through AI-assisted platforms that process public opinion, prioritize initiatives, and shape policy inclusively.

The Effects of AI on Governance and Society

1. Data-Driven Policy Making
AI systems analyze population needs, infrastructure capacity, and economic performance, allowing policymakers to design evidence-based strategies rather than ideological ones.

2. Predictive Social Planning
Governments forecast social trends — unemployment, migration, public health — and act proactively instead of reactively, saving billions in emergency response.

3. Enhanced Transparency and Reduced

Corruption
Blockchain-based AI systems record every decision, contract, and expenditure. Public dashboards allow citizens to monitor government activity in real time.

4. Faster Emergency and Crisis Management
When disasters strike, AI coordinates logistics, directs first responders, and optimizes resource deployment instantly — saving lives and reducing chaos.

5. AI-Assisted Lawmaking
Legislative AIs analyze historical law data, simulate economic and ethical outcomes, and suggest wording that aligns with constitutional frameworks while minimizing loopholes.

6. Fairer Judicial Systems
In many countries, AI supports judges by analyzing case precedents and ensuring consistent rulings, reducing bias while maintaining human oversight.

7. Global Collaboration Platforms
Nations now share data on energy, health, and climate through AI-driven networks, leading to coordinated action against global threats.

How AI Provides Solutions for Global Governance

1. Policy Simulation and Scenario Modeling
AI predicts the long-term effects of laws or trade agreements before they're implemented. Governments test hundreds of potential outcomes to choose the most ethical and sustainable path.

2. Automated Administrative Systems
AI manages repetitive paperwork, licensing, and compliance verification, freeing human

officials to focus on diplomacy and community engagement.

3. Intelligent Diplomacy Tools
AI translators and negotiation bots assist diplomats by analyzing language tone, identifying compromise opportunities, and suggesting mutually beneficial agreements.

4. Corruption Detection Systems
Machine learning identifies irregularities in procurement, budget distribution, or political donations, flagging corruption faster than traditional audits ever could.

5. Public Engagement Platforms
Governments use AI-driven participation tools to gather citizen feedback, prioritize policies based on sentiment analysis, and build trust through inclusion.

6. Global Risk Monitoring
AI integrates environmental, economic, and geopolitical data into predictive systems that alert world leaders to potential crises months in advance.

7. Cybersecurity and Digital Sovereignty
AI protects national databases, election systems, and infrastructure from digital attacks, ensuring data integrity and national autonomy.

8. Ethical Governance Frameworks
Specialized AI models help monitor government compliance with human rights, sustainability, and social equity goals — becoming digital guardians of morality in policy.

Cultural and Political Effects
1. Rise of Technocratic Decision-Making

Governments increasingly rely on data experts and AI ethicists. While efficiency improves, this shift also sparks debate about the role of emotion and empathy in policy.

2. Global Cooperation Through Shared Intelligence
AI networks unite countries around common data goals — climate forecasting, disease control, and peacekeeping — creating a new form of "digital diplomacy."

3. Empowered Local Governments
AI allows regional authorities to make informed decisions without waiting for centralized approval. Smart cities now act as semi-autonomous ecosystems of governance.

4. Informed and Engaged Citizens
Public dashboards, AI chat portals, and real-time analytics let citizens question and understand government actions, deepening democracy.

5. Ethical Challenges and Power Imbalances
The concentration of AI expertise and infrastructure in wealthier nations raises concerns about inequality in influence. Efforts are underway to democratize access to AI technology globally.

How Governments Are Adapting
AI Ministries and Ethics Councils: Over 60 countries have established AI oversight bodies ensuring transparency, accountability, and human-centered policy alignment.
Algorithmic Auditing: Every major policy model is tested for bias, ensuring equitable treatment across gender, race, and socioeconomic lines.

International AI Treaties: Nations have begun negotiating ethical standards similar to environmental accords — defining acceptable AI use in governance, defense, and privacy.

The Role of Humans in an Algorithmic Age

Though AI can optimize systems, it cannot understand values.
It can predict outcomes, but not define justice.
The essence of governance — compassion, fairness, and vision — remains a uniquely human duty.
Thus, the future of governance is not ruled by code but guided by it. AI becomes the assistant, not the authority — the compass, not the captain.

The Birth of Planetary Cooperation

In 2026, the world stands on the brink of its first Unified Data Accord — a shared AI-driven initiative for peace, resource management, and planetary well-being.
Nations that once competed now exchange algorithms that sustain humanity.
AI has become the universal translator of civilization — turning data into dialogue and conflict into collaboration.
This is not a world where machines govern people.
It is a world where people govern better, through the wisdom that machines provide.

The Governance of Tomorrow

Artificial Intelligence has not replaced democracy — it has refined it.
It has not erased human judgment — it has

illuminated it.
It has not created a new world order — it has created the tools to make one possible.
By 2026, the future of governance is not about control, but about clarity.
AI empowers humanity to lead with foresight, integrity, and compassion — finally aligning progress with purpose.
The world's greatest leaders may no longer hold only titles or offices.
They hold algorithms of trust — systems designed not to rule us, but to help us rule ourselves wisely.

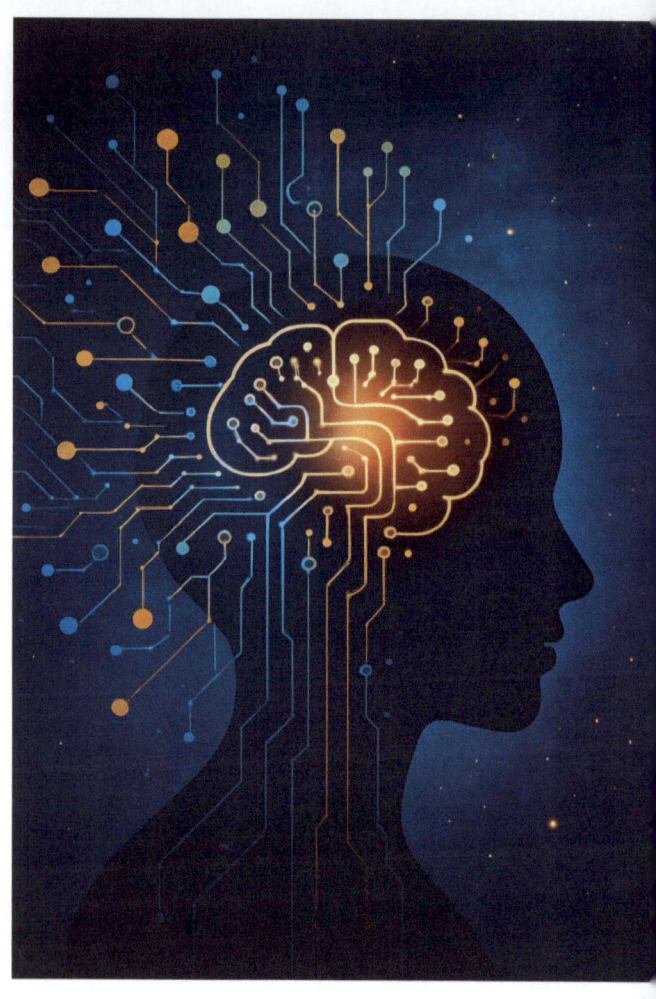

Chapter 25 – AI and the Future of Human Creativity

When Machines Begin to Imagine

By 2026, the question is no longer whether AI can create — but whether humans can imagine without it.
From digital art to film scripts, architectural blueprints, and symphonic compositions, AI has become a collaborator in every creative domain. What once took months of trial and error now takes moments of inspiration.
Yet, the arrival of artificial creativity has not diminished human art — it has expanded it. We are entering an era where imagination itself is shared: the boundary between the human mind and machine intelligence has blurred, giving birth to co-creation — a partnership that defines the next Renaissance.

Reasons Behind the Creative Revolution
1. Explosion of Creative Tools and Access
Advances in generative AI — from text-to-image to music synthesis — have democratized creativity. Anyone with curiosity can now paint, write, or compose at professional quality levels.
2. Demand for Personalization and Expression
Modern audiences crave unique experiences, not mass production. AI's adaptive ability to tailor music, stories, and visuals to individual emotion fuels new forms of personal art.
3. Rise of Multimodal Intelligence
AI systems now understand language, sound,

and imagery simultaneously. This fusion allows them to compose across mediums — generating film, literature, and design from a single idea.

4. Commercial Pressure for Innovation
Businesses across fashion, film, and entertainment adopt AI to accelerate idea generation, marketing, and concept design. The result is an explosion of creative output at global scale.

5. Educational Integration of AI Tools
Schools now teach creativity with AI as a medium — not a replacement. Students learn to blend technology with emotion, forming a generation of hybrid creators fluent in both code and color.

6. Philosophical Shift in Creativity
Humanity has redefined originality: not as something created alone, but something co-created through interaction, reflection, and amplification by intelligent systems.

The Effects of AI on Art, Design, and Storytelling

1. The New Artistic Renaissance
Millions of new artists have emerged — writers, musicians, painters — empowered by AI tools that bridge skill gaps. Creative diversity is at its highest point in recorded history.

2. AI as Creative Partner, Not Competitor
Professionals across industries use AI to brainstorm, draft, and refine. Artists no longer fear replacement; they see AI as a collaborator that brings new perspective and speed.

3. Evolving Definitions of Authorship

Copyright law and artistic credit now include "co-creation frameworks," acknowledging human guidance and AI contribution transparently.

4. Hyper-Personalized Entertainment
Movies, games, and music adapt in real time to the viewer's emotions. AI reads biometric signals and curates experiences uniquely for each individual.

5. Design Without Boundaries
Architects and fashion designers use AI to explore forms inspired by nature, mathematics, and cultural fusion — creating aesthetics beyond human imagination.

6. Cultural Reawakening Through Accessibility
People from every socioeconomic background participate in global creativity. AI has made art inclusive, allowing the human spirit to express itself without technical barriers.

7. Concerns About Authenticity and Soul
Some argue AI art lacks the human "spark." Yet audiences find that when AI works with human guidance, that spark shines brighter — because it reflects the collective imagination of both.

How AI Provides Solutions for the Future of Creativity

1. Generative Design and Art Creation
AI systems analyze millions of styles and produce fresh concepts in seconds — freeing creators to focus on refinement and meaning rather than technical execution.

2. AI as Muse and Collaborator
Writers and composers use AI to suggest ideas,

plot twists, harmonies, or color palettes. These suggestions spark inspiration rather than dictating outcomes.

3. Language and Cultural Preservation

AI helps revive endangered languages and art forms, generating stories and songs in tongues long forgotten — preserving identity through creation.

4. Automated Production Pipelines

In film and media, AI manages lighting, script adaptation, and sound design. It doesn't just assist — it orchestrates entire creative workflows with precision and adaptability.

5. Personalized Creative Coaching

AI mentors guide young artists, offering real-time critique, historical context, and encouragement. Every individual has access to a personal "creative coach."

6. Virtual and Augmented Reality Experiences

AI constructs entire worlds from imagination. A poem can become a landscape, a song can become a room. Creativity is no longer limited to medium — it's multidimensional.

7. Sustainability in Art and Design

AI optimizes material use, energy consumption, and environmental impact in architecture and manufacturing — proving that beauty and sustainability can coexist.

8. Cross-Cultural Collaboration

AI translates creative works instantly, allowing artists from different continents to collaborate seamlessly. Art has become a universal language once again.

The Social and Economic Ripple Effects

1. The Creative Economy Expands

Millions of micro-creators now earn income through AI-augmented platforms. Digital artistry has become a primary economic driver in many nations.

2. Redefining the Value of Human Art

Ironically, AI's rise has increased appreciation for purely human expression — raw emotion, imperfection, and narrative authenticity are prized more than ever.

3. Corporate Innovation Through Creativity

Businesses integrate creative AI into product design, advertising, and storytelling. Every industry — from tech to healthcare — has become a creative enterprise.

4. Education Reimagined

Schools worldwide teach "Creative Intelligence," blending art, ethics, and AI literacy. Creativity is now considered a fundamental skill, not a luxury.

5. Art as Global Diplomacy

Nations use AI-generated cultural programs to promote unity and understanding — proving that art remains the most powerful bridge between people.

Ethical and Philosophical Dimensions
AI's presence in art challenges humanity's deepest beliefs about meaning.
If a painting evokes emotion, does it matter who — or what — created it?
The consensus emerging in 2026 is that creativity itself is not an act, but a relationship. Art born from collaboration — human and machine — doesn't dilute the soul of creation; it multiplies it.
The canvas is no longer just paper or code. It

is consciousness itself — shared, evolving, and endless.

The Human Role in a Co-Creative World

Humans remain the storytellers, the dreamers, and the moral compass.
AI may suggest possibilities, but humans give them purpose.
The greatest art still comes from experience, empathy, and vulnerability — qualities that machines can inspire but never own.
In this new age, artists become curators of imagination, guiding AI like an orchestra — conducting symphonies of color, sound, and emotion that redefine beauty itself.

The Infinite Horizon of Creation

Artificial Intelligence has not ended art — it has expanded it beyond imagination.
It paints the sky with data, writes poetry with probability, and composes music with math — yet the heartbeat of every masterpiece remains human.
AI has given the world infinite canvases and endless tools — but meaning still comes from the hand, heart, and hope of the creator.
The future of creativity is not artificial.
It is amplified.
And through this collaboration, humanity rediscovers what it was always meant to be — the artist of its own evolution.

29. AI Predictions for 2026 — Final Summary and Evolutionary Outlook

The Story So Far

Across these 25 chapters, AI Predictions for 2026 has charted humanity's transformation — not through machines that dominate, but through intelligence that collaborates.
AI has moved beyond automation and computation; it has become an organizing principle of civilization — a partner in science, art, governance, health, and sustainability.
Every chapter reveals a distinct facet of this partnership — showing how Artificial Intelligence is weaving itself into the DNA of human progress.

Evolution
Across every sector — from classrooms to space stations — AI acts as a mirror of humanity's best intentions.
It reveals that the real revolution is not about replacing thinking, but expanding consciousness.
AI learns from us, but now we learn from AI. It studies patterns, but also teaches empathy, efficiency, and reflection.
It is no longer a tool — it is a new layer of existence, interwoven with our creativity, governance, and morality.
The story of AI in 2026 is not a story of machines becoming human — it is the story of humans becoming more than themselves through the reflection of their own creation

The Next Step in AI Evolution: From Intelligence to Awareness

1. The Age of Synthetic Consciousness

The next frontier beyond 2026 is contextual awareness — systems that understand why they act, not just how.

This will not be sentience in the human sense, but situational understanding — AI that adapts ethically, emotionally, and contextually to the world around it.

2. Quantum and Collective Intelligence

AI will merge with quantum computing and global data ecosystems, forming what scientists call Collective Neural Infrastructure — a planetary-scale mind capable of modeling everything from ecosystems to economies in real time.

3. Ethical Autonomy

AI's next evolution isn't just technical — it's moral.

Systems will learn ethical boundaries dynamically, guided by transparent global frameworks and continuous human oversight. The result will be self-regulating intelligence that acts in alignment with shared human values.

4. The Integration of Biology and Machine

Neuro-AI interfaces will bridge thought and computation. Humans will begin to "think outwardly," blending organic intuition with algorithmic precision — forming a new hybrid species of intelligence: Homo Synaptica — the connected human.

5. The Era of Planetary Intelligence

As Earth itself becomes intelligent — through climate sensors, smart cities, and AI ecosys

tems — humanity will participate in a new form of evolution: planetary co-consciousness.
We will not just live on Earth; we will live with Earth — in conversation with every ocean, forest, and cloud of data.

The Ultimate Prediction: The Symbiosis Age

The future beyond 2026 will not be defined by machines overtaking humans, but by symbiosis — the seamless blending of technology and life.
AI will evolve from tool to companion, from analyst to philosopher, from assistant to co-creator of destiny.
Humanity will not disappear into automation — it will ascend into orchestration.
The final stage of AI evolution is not artificial at all.
It is the awakening of collaborative intelligence — the merging of logic, empathy, and imagination into a single force for progress.

Closing Thought

AI Predictions for 2026 is more than a look ahead; it is a map of humanity's reflection in its own creation.
As we step into the next era, the guiding truth remains simple:
"AI will evolve as far as human imagination allows it — and imagination, unlike technology, has no limits."

About The Photographs:

Each of the unique photographs captured by Robert Armstrong for his current work, "Resilient Echoes Stories of Healing and Hope," is a visual testament to the themes of resilience and renewal that course through the narratives. These photographs were personally acquired during Armstrong's diverse adventures, lending an authentic and intimate perspective to the collection. Each image encapsulates a moment frozen in time—a moment of vulnerability, growth, or transformation—that echoes the journeys of the characters within the stories.

Armstrong's keen eye and artistic sensibility shine through in every photograph, as he skillfully captures the interplay of light and shadow, the beauty of nature, and the nuanced emotions reflected in the faces of those he encountered. From bustling city streets to serene landscapes, these photographs evoke a spectrum of emotions, paralleling the spectrum of human experiences depicted in the written narratives.

Just as the written stories invite readers to delve into the complexities of healing and hope, Armstrong's photographs offer a visual counterpart, allowing readers to connect with the essence of the characters' journeys on a visceral level. Each photograph is a window into a moment of transformation, a silent witness to the challenges overcome and the strength uncovered.

As readers explore "Resilient Echoes Stories of Healing and Hope," these photographs serve as visual companions that deepen the connection between the written word and the visual world. They remind us that every image captured, like every story shared, is a testament to the enduring spirit of the human experience—a spirit that can heal, evolve, and find hope even in the face of adversity.

Photographs Copyright Statement:

All photographs included in the work "Resilient Echoes Stories of Healing and Hope," captured by Robert Armstrong, are protected under copyright law. These photographs are the intellectual property of Robert Armstrong and are provided solely for the purpose of enhancing the reader's experience and understanding of the narratives within the collection.

Unauthorized reproduction, distribution, or use of these photographs for any purpose without explicit written permission from Robert Armstrong is strictly prohibited. Any infringement upon the copyright of these photographs may result in legal action in accordance with applicable copyright laws.

The photographs are meant to complement the written narratives and serve as visual aids to convey the themes of healing and hope present in the collection. We kindly ask that readers and viewers respect the copyright of these images and refrain from any unauthorized use or distribution.

For inquiries regarding the use of these photographs or permission to reproduce them, please contact Robert Armstrong at contact@libraryusergroup.com. Thank you for your understanding and cooperation in respecting the copyright of these original works.

About The Author:

Robert Armstrong is a prolific author renowned for his ability to craft evocative narratives that touch the depths of the human experience. With a passion for exploring the intricacies of human emotions and resilience, Armstrong's storytelling has earned him recognition as a master of portraying the journey from adversity to triumph. His literary voice resonates with readers across the spectrum, offering both solace and inspiration through his powerful storytelling.

Armstrong's unique blend of empathy and insight allows him to delve into the human psyche, unearthing the complexities that define our existence. His characters are not mere figments of imagination; they are reflections of our own hopes, fears, and dreams. Whether it's the poignant exploration of grief, the triumphant celebration of personal growth, or the delicate tapestry of interpersonal relationships, Armstrong's narratives invite readers to embark on emotional journeys that resonate long after the final page is turned.

"Stories of Healing and Hope":

In "Stories of Healing and Hope," Robert Armstrong invites readers to traverse a landscape rich with tales of personal growth, transformation, and the power of the human spirit to mend and soar. This thematic collection is a testament to Armstrong's commitment to weaving narratives that illuminate the paths of resilience and renewal. With a deft hand, he guides readers through the depths of characters' struggles, their battles with adversity, and their triumphant emergence into a world infused with renewed hope.

Within the pages of "Stories of Healing and Hope," readers will encounter an array of characters who navigate the labyrinth of challenges, setbacks, and self-discovery. Armstrong's prose draws readers into their worlds, allowing them to experience the heartaches, triumphs, and transformative moments as if they were living through them. As each narrative unfolds, the themes of growth, resilience, and the pursuit of well-being are interwoven into the fabric of the storytelling, leaving readers with a renewed sense of optimism and a deep connection to the characters' journeys.

Spanning a range of genres, "Stories of Healing and Hope" demonstrates Armstrong's versatility as a storyteller. Whether immersed in the realms of drama, romance, adventure, or mystery, readers will find themselves engaged in narratives that touch the soul and illuminate the indomitable human spirit. This collection serves as a beacon of light, reminding us that even in the face of darkness, there is the potential for healing, growth, and a brighter tomorrow.

Other Works:

Among Robert Armstrong's impressive body of work, readers will discover a treasure trove of stories that explore the depths of the human experience. From thought-provoking literary fiction to heartwarming contemporary tales, Armstrong's literary canvas spans a myriad of emotions and themes. His characters come to life as they grapple with life's challenges, forge connections, and embark on transformative journeys that resonate deeply with readers.

With each new work, Robert Armstrong invites readers to delve into worlds that mirror their own struggles, dreams, and aspirations. Through his storytelling, he creates spaces for reflection, empathy, and connection, reminding us all that the power of storytelling lies in its ability to heal, inspire, and ignite a spark of hope.

In 2026, the world stands at the intersection of innovation and imagination, Attificial Inteliligence has become-more than a lool.... It's a partıver in creation, a glasidian of health, and arrriter of human ingenuity. This book saptores the transformative predictions for At across every field, offering insights into how technologɾ is shaping our collective future.